BEYOND EDUCATION

ALAN M. THOMAS

BEYOND EDUCATION

A New Perspective on Society's Management of Learning

Jossey-Bass Publishers

San Francisco • Oxford • 1991

BEYOND EDUCATION
A New Perspective on Society's Management of Learning
   by Alan M. Thomas

Copyright © 1991 by: Jossey-Bass Inc., Publishers
                     350 Sansome Street
                     San Francisco, California 94104
                              &
                     Jossey-Bass Limited
                     Headington Hill Hall
                     Oxford OX3 0BW

Library of Congress Cataloging-in-Publication Data

Thomas, Alan M.
   Beyond education : a new perspective on society's management of
learning / Alan M. Thomas. — 1st ed.
      p.   cm. — (The Jossey-Bass higher and adult education series)
   Includes bibliographical references and index.
   ISBN 1-55542-311-6 (alk. paper)
   1. Learning.   2. Education — Social aspects.   I. Title.
II. Series.
LB1060.T5   1991
370.19 — dc20   90-48584
                                                              CIP

Manufactured in the United States of America

The paper in this book meets the guidelines for
permanence and durability of the Committee on
Production Guidelines for Book Longevity of
the Council on Library Resources.

JACKET DESIGN BY WILLI BAUM

FIRST EDITION

Code 9113

The Jossey-Bass
Higher and Adult Education Series

Consulting Editor
Adult and Continuing Education

Alan B. Knox
University of Wisconsin, Madison

Contents

To Jo Anne,
who always believed;
to Alan, Matthew, Rachel, and Martha,
with whom learning was the watchword;
and to Jeanie Stewart,
who never let me down

Preface

In August 1945 I was seventeen years old. I thus completed my adolescence at about the same moment as did the world. From that time on, I became aware that any generation of adults held the survival of all of us in their hands. The choices they would make, the actions they would take, would arise inescapably from what they knew or did not know, what they had learned, and, most important, what they were learning. Since that time the generation of adults holding power has changed, and the threat of despoiling the environment has to some extent replaced the threat of atomic war. The importance of learning in determining the actions not only of those in power but of all the world's citizens has not diminished, however. On the contrary, it has increased.

The reader will notice that I said learning, not education. One of the main arguments of *Beyond Education* is that learning and education are not the same thing and that the distinction between them is vital. Unfortunately, that distinction has been forgotten during most of this century.

When the British author H. G. Wells stated just before the century's beginning that the future of humankind would be determined by the outcome of a race between education and catastrophe, most of the world agreed with him. The first two-thirds of the century therefore saw a race among the nations of the world to see which could build the biggest, most inclusive system of formal education. This effort reached a peak in the years just after World War II. During that time there were

fierce debates about many aspects of education, but the value
of formal education and the limited set of learning objectives
that it supported was never questioned. "If it isn't taught, it isn't
worth learning" became the implicit slogan of the period.

Only in the 1970s and 1980s, with the advent of the so-
called information society, did disillusion and doubt about the
efficacy of existing systems of formal education begin to appear.
Critics noted that even though people were spending more years
in formal education than ever before, education systems did not
seem to be either fulfilling their traditional roles or making much
contribution to solving pressing world problems such as unemployment, poverty, and war.

This book is, in part, an attempt to understand the sources
of this disillusionment and to suggest ways to counteract the
malaise that has overtaken formal education. I do not wish to
attack the formal educational system or to minimize its un-
doubted contributions to individual and social well-being. I
merely wish to point out its limits. I hope to strengthen the
educational system by identifying both what it can do well and
what can be done better through other means of supporting
learning.

Primarily, however, this is a book about learning. I have
devoted a lifetime to the education of adults, and I therefore
have been in an excellent position to observe the extraordinary
human potential for learning. I have witnessed the emergence
of learning in unexpected places, brought about by unconventional means, and producing quite unexpected results. The mar-
gins of formal education, where most of my work has been done,
have proven to be good places from which to achieve a perspective on that colossal enterprise and to see, however dimly, the
larger domain of learning of which formal education is only a
part.

All people learn, and they are capable of doing so throughout their lives. Learning reaches far beyond the books and classes
of formal education, extending deep into the fabric of our everyday social existence; indeed, much of our most important learning takes place outside the education system. Today we are redis-
covering the incalculable social and political significance of

learning. This book explores that significance for us as individuals and for the groups, communities, nations, and societies in which we live.

All human groups, from family to huge corporation and from neighborhood to nation-state, must respond to individuals' need and potential for learning. Responding to learning needs and potential means managing learning. The management of learning, in turn, means the ordering of the decisions that all individuals and groups must make as they struggle to cope with changes in their environment.

We all attempt to meet our needs, and when a change in our environment causes an old method of meeting a need to become ineffective, that unmet need becomes a learning need: that is, we need to learn a new way to produce the old result. For individuals, management of learning means defining learning needs and then trying to find the best way to satisfy them. For governments, management of learning means making decisions that answer the key questions of who is (or ought to be) learning what, under what circumstances, at whose expense, and to what end. The traditional way of managing learning has been through formal education, but this is not the only or even often the best way. We need to understand alternative methods of learning management in order to make better use of educational resources and find the most productive avenues for meeting our learning goals.

Governments have always had to manage learning, but today the need for deliberate, intelligent learning management is becoming ever more vital to governments and individual citizens alike. In this age of rapid technological development, modern societies are constantly changing, which means that their members face a need for constant and lifelong learning. Increasing numbers of adults in those societies are demanding help in meeting this need. Governments, in turn, are trying to find ways to meet that demand and at the same time struggling to deal with the turbulence and unpredictable outcomes that arise in societies in which most of the members are learning most of the time. The governments of today face the challenge of managing learning on an unprecedented scale.

In addition to considering the relationship between learning and education and describing alternative approaches to the management of learning, this book uses learning as a perspective from which to examine the time and societies in which we live. I believe that not only matters traditionally associated with education but virtually all sociopolitical activities can be illuminated from this perspective. I will use a learning perspective to describe some of what is now happening in the world and how these events and attitudes came about. I will also provide a framework or template that can be used to analyze the dynamics of any society or group in terms of the choices it has made or is making about the management of its members' learning.

Who Should Read This Book

This book is directed first of all to educators in the hope that it will help them understand what is happening to their enterprise and what its limitations and possibilities are. I have offered suggestions for redefining formal education's role in modern society in a way that takes fuller cognizance of the growing population of mature students and establishes a better working relationship with agencies and sources of learning outside the formal education system.

Sociologists, historians, and students of related disciplines may also find this book interesting. It will be particularly relevant to those who want to learn more about the social history of learning and education. However, as I explain in Chapter Seven, any society or group can be analyzed profitably from a learning perspective. I provide a framework for doing this and offer examples to show how the framework can be used to understand particular social developments, compare societies, and contrast the activities of the same society during different time periods.

Finally, I hope this book will reach some general readers as well. I believe that any thoughtful citizen can gain insights into our modern world, including both the problems that bedevil it and hopes for its future enlightenment, by viewing it from a learning perspective. By discovering the central but often unappreciated part that learning plays in public and private life, individuals can learn to manage their own learning better and also have a more critical understanding of decisions made by others that will affect their learning.

Organization of the Book

Chapters One and Two are introductory chapters. Chapter One examines the concept of learning, particularly the characteristics of learning that have social and political significance, and explains the difference between learning and education. Chapter Two sets learning and education in their social and historical context and explores the relationship between the two.

Chapter Three presents a "learning map" or diagram that can help in understanding learning management decisions made by individuals and groups. The chapter describes the three "domains" pictured on the map (the Social, Learning, and Educational domains) and also discusses the contrasting roles characteristic of the different domains (citizen, learner, group member, and student).

Learning needs arise all the time, but those needs are likely to become especially intense during certain "learning moments." Chapter Four considers the learning moments of entry, life passages, societywide changes, and special circumstances (the handling of people with special challenges or handicaps). It discusses how governments and other groups have tried to cope with the learning needs associated with each kind of learning moment and what effects followed their different responses.

Societies and their governments (or smaller groups and their leaders) can respond to individual or group learning needs by permitting, encouraging, directing, or forbidding learning aimed at certain objectives. Chapters Five and Six consider these different responses and their consequences. Chapter Five describes methods and effects of permitting, forbidding, and, especially, encouraging or supporting learning. Chapter Six focuses on directing learning through formal educational systems, considering the various elements of such systems and pointing out contradictions within formal education as it is at present conceived.

Chapter Seven presents a framework through which any society or group can be analyzed from a learning perspective. The chapter explains how the framework can be used to study a particular society at a certain point in time, compare two societies, or compare the activities of a particular society during different time periods to reveal its dynamics.

Chapter Eight concludes the book by offering recommendations for modifying our approaches to learning management and redesigning the formal educational system. Through changes that emphasize a closer relationship between the learning that takes place outside the educational system and that which takes place inside, I believe we can create a true system of continuing education and, even more important, a "learning society" in which all citizens can fulfill their potential for lifelong learning.

If we are to attain any of our individual or collective aspirations, we must find ways to nourish and celebrate learning and fully develop our learning potential, for all significant attempts to solve social problems inevitably involve learning. Indeed, the very survival of our world today depends on successful learning and successful management of learning. *Beyond Education* will, I hope, offer suggestions that can help us to achieve that success.

Toronto, Ontario   Alan M. Thomas
December 1990

The Author

Alan M. Thomas is a professor of adult education and former chairman of the Department of Adult Education at the Ontario Institute for Studies in Education in Toronto. He received his B.A. degree (1949) in English and philosophy from the University of Toronto; his M.A. degree (1953) in the history of education from Teachers College, Columbia University; and his Ph.D. degree (1964) in social psychology from Teachers College.

Thomas has been assistant professor of education at the University of British Columbia, executive director of the Canadian Association for Adult Education, and executive assistant to the Canadian government's Minister for Communications. He also was the director of the first Global Symposium on Learning (Toronto, 1985), which was supported by the United Nations University and the Canadian International Development Agency. This symposium resulted in the publication *Learning and Development*, which Thomas coauthored with Edward Ploman (1986).

Thomas is a member of the Order of Canada (1983) and holds an honorary diploma from Humber College, Toronto. His research activities have included studies of adult education in industry, labor education in Canada, education in Canadian federal prisons, and the use of experiential learning in Canadian education. His most recent work has focused on studies of the interaction between learning and the law.

BEYOND
EDUCATION

 **1**

Learning:
Its Significance
to Society

All organisms spend their lives trying to meet their needs. The *Oxford Illustrated Dictionary* (1975) defines need as "necessity arising from circumstances of case; imperative demand for presence or possession; thing wanted, respect in which want is felt, requirement." The most basic need is the need for survival. This fundamental need, as Maslow (1954) and others (for example, Illich, 1971) have pointed out, breaks up into infinite numbers of subsidiary needs, such as those for food, shelter, body covering, and contact with other beings of one's kind. Maslow noted that needs may be emotional or spiritual as well as material or physical; the needs for food and shelter do not differ in kind from the needs for love and aesthetic experience.

Learning can be considered to be a need. It is also the means of satisfying all other needs. Whenever the environment of human beings changes, the daily pursuit of the satisfaction of needs is interrupted because knowledge and skills already possessed no longer serve to satisfy a particular need. A once-common game animal dies out, for example, or a new one appears, making old hunting skills ineffective; climate changes blight one food crop or encourage another, and farmers must change their ways. Environmental changes translate other needs, such as the need for food, into learning needs.

When familiar methods no longer produce familiar effects,

1

new methods must be found that will produce the old result, (or another that meets the need in question equally well). This means that one or more individuals must learn something that they have not known before. It may or may not be something that no human being has ever known before. The people faced with (or seeking) a new game animal must learn new hunting skills. If they succeed, other people in their group will have to learn new skills in tanning, curing, cooking, and so on in order to deal with the new animal.

Even attempts to remove a learning challenge by removing the environmental change or novel stimulus that produced it require some change in behavior and therefore some new learning. If, for example, the hunters decide to avoid the challenge of learning how to hunt a new game animal by following their familiar prey as it migrates to a new climate area, they simply trade the need to learn new hunting skills for the need to learn to live in a different land.

People have always had learning needs, but these needs have increased greatly today. For most of recorded history, the environment in which human beings lived was determined primarily by natural events. During the past three centuries, however, that environment has become more and more subject to technological control by governments and other large organizations. The harnessing of atomic power in the 1940s provided the most spectacular example of that control and its dangers, but the Greenhouse Effect and other current specters of environmental destruction are just as threatening even if more subtle. In short, the environment has become more subject to control by human decision, and acquiring the learning that will allow us to make such decisions wisely has become vital. Our learning determines our behavior, and as our behavior has become all-important to the survival of our planet, so has our learning. Indeed, we have discovered that we need to continue learning throughout our lives.

The Meaning of Learning: Two Views

Perhaps because learning is so personal, the word and concept of learning have been given many interpretations and uses. The older and more traditional view of learning (the one held by Francis Bacon in 1674, for example), and the one prevalent in almost all education theory as well as in some contemporary psychological writings such as that of Botkin, Elmandjra, and Maritza (1979), sees learning in terms of its objectives or outcomes. Writers who view learning in this way sometimes seem to possess a degree of intellectual imperialism (might one say "educationism"?) in that they appear to intend that the learning objectives they favor and the language in which these objectives are expressed should constitute the "one true way" in which learning is conceived. They often imply a value for certain learning outcomes without knowing whether that is what these outcomes mean to the learner and without clarifying the ideological system from which that value arises. To people with this view, learning is primarily a noun, as in "He is a man of much learning." Learning is a sort of intangible possession that people work to acquire.

To most classical learning theorists (for example, Pavlov [1960], Thorndike [1935], and Skinner [1953]), however, as well as to more contemporary contributors such as Mezirow (1978), Lovell (1980), and Schon (1971), learning is basically a verb. It is an action, a process. These scientists are less concerned with the outcomes of learning than with the way learning is accomplished. Their view of learning is the one we espouse in this book.

Both views of learning are legitimate and useful, but the distinction between them is important. Each view has significant sociopolitical implications. When learning is seen as being important only in terms of some specific set of objectives, rather than as a process that is valuable in itself, a considerable potential threat to the fabric of democratic society exists. Totalitarian societies and organizations deliberately maintain such a view of learning. So, albeit with a less obviously authoritarian stance, do systems of formal education. They select some learning objectives as important and associate all successful learning with these objectives. Learning undergone in pursuit of other objectives is disregarded. Western school systems, for example, reward learning associated with literacy, technology, individualism, and self-reliance but tend to ignore learning associated with mysticism, cooperation, or self-abnegation. People who persist in seeking the latter learning outcomes usually are regarded as eccentrics or failures. Once our belief in our capacity to learn is measured only by our ability to learn certain things, an essential individual freedom and power has been lost.

Characteristics of Learning in a Social Context

Since human beings are social beings, all characteristics of learning can be said to have some social consequences. Certain characteristics, however, seem more salient in a social context than others. We will discuss these characteristics and their implications in this chapter. Some will be reexamined in Chapter Eight. The characteristics of learning that seem most important in social affairs are the following:

- Learning is action.
- Learning is individual.
- Learning is influenced by other people.
- Learning is a response to stimuli.
- Learning is lifelong.
- Learning is irreversible.
- Learning takes time.
- Learning cannot be coerced.

All of these characteristics are relatively familiar to readers of psychological or educational theory. They seldom have been considered outside the context of these fields, however, and even within that context, they are often ignored or taken for granted. We believe that modern societies are affected by these characteristics of learning in all spheres of public policy. For example, unemployment is frequently the result of a mismatch between individual skills and available jobs. When unemployment occurs on a large scale, opportunities for adult workers to learn new skills must be provided. Like all learning, as we will show, that learning will require time, supports of various kinds, and the will of the learners.

Learning Is Action. First of all, we share the view that learning is a verb: it is an activity, it is doing. The now-legendary battle cry of John Dewey and the progressive educators of the early part of this century, "learning by doing," was perhaps an inevitable rebellion against the ideal picture of public education at the time: millions of pupils sitting quietly and obediently in their places while information was delivered to them in measured doses. Dewey advocated a type of instruction that encouraged many forms of student activity as the means for learning what the schools were trying to teach. The only trouble with his slogan is that it implies that some form of learning that does *not* involve doing is possible, which does not seem to be the case.

What we have learned (and what we have not learned) determines our actions, and our actions in turn help us learn. If a government wishes to restrict learning about some subject or area of life, all it needs to do is reduce the possibilities of action with respect to that subject. A citizen cannot really learn how to participate in a country's government, for example, unless he or she can take action concerning that government at regular intervals by voting.

As an action, learning both requires and releases energy. People who are actively engaged in learning also appear to have more energy for other activities than people who are not. We are commonly impressed with the energy of the young, but we seldom reflect on the fact that such energy may be a consequence of the amount of time they devote to learning rather than merely of the fact that they are young. Evidence from studies of older learners supports this idea: older people who are willing to learn also seem to show more energy for other things. In this light it is difficult to understand the preference of employers for hiring employees who already "know" their jobs when, within some limits, the benefits that arise from the energy and loyalty generated by an employee who is eager and flexible enough to learn a new job are likely to be very much greater.

Because learning is action, learning can help one take an active role in life and "make one's own luck." An old Yorkshire proverb states, "When land is gone and money's spent, learning is most excellent." One possible interpretation of this proverb is that a person who lacks both land and money may still use learning—that is, intelligence and capacity for learning—to find ways to survive and even live well.

A similar admiration for the active stance suggested by learning may explain some of the respect that middle-class societies, with their focus on individual achievement rather than inherited wealth or power, grant to the "professions." This group of occupations requires lifelong learning from its members and bases its rewards upon active application of skill, knowledge, and judgment in service to society. The professional represents the most powerful of the visions of institutionalized lifelong learning. Fortunately, this vision is now being extended to many other people and occupations in modern society.

Learning Is Individual. Only individuals can learn, and our individual learning makes us who we are. We are the sum of everything we have learned, and we are also manifestations of the way we have gone about that learning (Kolb, 1984; Jacobs and Fuhrman, 1984). Furthermore, learning is the bridge between who we are and who we hope to (or at least who we will) become. Every time we learn something independently, we reinvent ourselves.

Learning anything, no matter how trivial, transforms a person. Because we are the total of all we have learned, a "new person" is created with each act of learning, even if the "new" differs from the "old" only by, say, the knowledge of the new telephone number of a friend who has moved. The difference in that case is insignificant for practical purposes, but the change caused by other types of learning—learning how to love a new partner, for example—can be profound. It can even be so intense as to result in what James (1961) calls "conversion."

Learning, at least in the way human beings do it, can be said to be a uniquely human characteristic. To be sure, recent research on many kinds of living things has thrown doubt on the formerly popular view that only human beings can learn at all (Holland, 1986). Even bacteria, the simplest of organisms, appear capable of "learning" to some extent; that is, they can change their behavior in response to a change in their environment (Pietsch, 1983). Higher animals such as apes can learn, and even invent, quite complex behaviors, including some involving the use of tools or language, although interpretation of these behaviors remains controversial (Smullen, 1978; Linden, 1976; Benderly, 1980). Nonetheless, conscious learning and its direction toward particular predetermined objectives remains a distinctive and indeed dominant feature of individual human beings.

Stress on the individual nature of learning and other activities is often said, with some justification, to be primarily a Western view, but it is not exclusively so. Buddhism, for example, also holds that learning is confined to the individual. Buddhists believe, in fact, that an individual's learning continues through multiple lives (Hewage, 1986; Ariyaratne, 1986).

Many contemporary writers have discussed so-called "group learning" or "organizational learning." We believe, however, that any claim that groups learn, except in a metaphorical sense, not only robs the term *learning* of most of its precise meaning but can be seen as a threat to the idea of individual responsibility that is a keystone of Western democratic societies. The founders of liberal democratic states insisted on the association of one person with one vote because they believed that ultimate political power should rest with that one self-sustaining, learning entity, the individual human being (Beer, 1966).

The legal systems of most societies, especially most Western societies, similarly are based on individual responsibility, with its implication of individual learning. The idea of a corporation as a "person" is a convenient legal fiction, and corporations can be held responsible for certain acts in civil law, but the ultimate responsibility for the actions of a corporation remains with the individuals who compose it. The law both insists on individual responsibility and uses the human potential for learning by applying various methods that "encourage" people who engage in behavior that has been deemed objectionable to learn to alter that behavior. To say that groups can learn is to risk denying individual responsibility for learning and therefore for behavior.

We know instinctively that we differ from our peers in what we have learned and are learning and in how we go about the process of learning, but schools, with their focus on groups, deny most of that individuality. Pursuit of individual learning objectives by collective means such as schools and classes is a principal characteristic of educational systems. The existence of this organizational arrangement suggests that everyone does, or at least should, learn at the same rate and in the same way. Instead of helping us understand that we are what we have learned, education encourages us to conclude that we are merely what we have been taught. We are provided with little help in understanding the learning process or our individual approach to that process. If we do remain aware of learning differences, that awareness leads us to form attitudes about our learning capacity that often last a lifetime and can help or hinder us in everything we do.

Learning Is Influenced by Other People. Although a group cannot learn, members of the group can, and their learning can have powerful effects on other group members and on the group as a whole. Groups can have equally powerful effects on individual learning.

Learning is a multiplier. Each individual is both a transmitter and a receiver of continuous stimuli for and from other individuals. Every action, physical or verbal, of one person provides a model of behavior that can be learned by someone else. In this sense, everyone is both teacher and learner all through life. People are very aware of the fact that children both learn from and provide models for others, but they tend to forget that this is true of adults as well. Indeed, we cannot overemphasize that adults learn more (both positive and negative) from other adults than from any other single source, and by a very wide margin.

Particularly powerful models of behavior are provided by those who (by virtue of their personalities, their social or political position, or both) act as leaders. In groups in which government is defined primarily by the personalities of those in power rather than by a constitutional framework — in which, in other words, personal power and political power are virtually synonymous — there is no such thing as a deposed leader being merely "out of office." For as long as deposed rulers live, they influence others and therefore potentially threaten the state; therefore people who fall from power usually are executed or at least exiled by their successors. This has been true in tribal societies, in which public and private life are not clearly distinguished, and in many so-called "civilized" societies as well. Royal siblings in many early societies were expected to fight for the throne, and the winner killed, mutilated, or exiled the rest. Elizabeth I of England could not be content with merely imprisoning Mary Queen of Scots; she felt she had to have her cousin executed because the deposed queen, whether willingly or not, was a constant focus of rebellions against Elizabeth's throne. We can observe this situation in less bloody form today in many small groups in our society in which leadership is strongly equated with personal power: leaders out of power usually leave the group, thus ending the likelihood that they will threaten the existing leadership by providing models of alternative or competitive goals and practices from which group members can learn.

Learning Is a Response to Stimuli. Psychologists and others who have studied learning have had different opinions about whether learning is a drive (that is, an inward pressure impelling, if not compelling, a person to deliberate acts) or strictly a response to external stimuli. Evidence from the study of animals seems to suggest an unstable balance between the need for novelty and the need for security (Ardrey, 1966). On the one hand, an animal tries to establish control over its territory, which increases security but cuts down on novelty and stimulation; on the other hand, the animal eventually leaves this "safe" territory even if all its physical needs are being met there, apparently in search of novelty, challenge, and new learning. This implies that learning derives from internal needs comparable to those for food, shelter, and affection. The alternative is to believe that the stimulus to learn comes from outside the organism, usually in the form of an unsolved problem presented by the environment.

The natural propensity of children and adolescents to learn tends to be taken for granted. Certainly it has been used to justify investing a great deal of money and effort in directing their learning toward socially acceptable objectives. An unfortunate consequence of this automatic acceptance has been the equally automatic acceptance of the idea that the "drive" for learning diminishes as chronological age advances, except in a few gifted people.

It may be, however, that the apparent drive for learning observed in children comes from the fact that their relationship to their environment is changing relentlessly because of their physical and cognitive growth. If your arm is longer today than it was six months or a year ago, you have some new problems to solve in your physical relationship with your environment. The complexities of the growth that takes place during the first seventeen or eighteen years of life present innumerable physical and psychological conundrums that must be coped with, and young people must therefore learn constantly, whether they intentionally set out to do so or not. It thus seems likely that the initial impulse toward learning is a response both to the demands of growth and to stimuli in the environment.

Learning Is Lifelong. Since learning is cumulative and irreversible, by the time the rapid changes related to physical growth have slowed, a person has developed a number of attitudes, skills, and habits associated with coping with problems presented by a changing environment—that is, with learning. If the attitudes are positive and the skills successful, an adult is likely not only to go on learning when forced to do so by circumstances but also to seek out new stimuli to respond to and learn from.

For most people, learning becomes more closely attached to particular objectives as life progresses, and they become indifferent to learning of other subjects or for other purposes. Some people, however, remain much more curious and willing to learn than others. People can and do engage in the activity of learning throughout their lives. Recent studies in gerontology have emphasized the human potential for lifelong learning (Lovell, 1980; MacLeish, 1976).

The adage that "you cannot teach an old dog new tricks" no longer finds public favor, although policies seemingly based on this idea, such as compulsory retirement, still invest many areas of public life (Baum, 1974). Some reflection on this homily, however, reveals a deeper truth. The statement argues that old dogs cannot be *taught* new tricks, but it does not claim that they cannot *learn* them. Perhaps, in fact, it is precisely where maturity meets formal education that the real distinction between learning and education finds its most significant modern expression.

Maturity could be said to lie not in living for a certain number of years but in a person's development of the ability to control and direct his or her own learning. This development occurs when experience allows the person both to identify the subjects about which he or she wishes to learn and to plan the approach by which that learning will best be achieved. When a mature person encounters a formal educational agency that tries to force him or her to submit to predetermined decisions about what should be learned and how, some sort of dialogue, if not outright conflict, is bound to result. Less enlightened agencies and instructors try to ignore or suppress this dialogue, but the more enlightened ones welcome it.

Because of contemporary society's growing dependence on the learning capacity of citizens of all ages, policies that curb or obstruct the learning of older citizens are being reexamined, albeit slowly. The present arguments over both the justice and the economic efficiency of compulsory retirement are examples of that reexamination. There is a new conflict of opinion, however, over whether what older people learn is significant to society as a whole. A brief exploration of current educational programs for older adults suggests that many are mere busywork, offered more as "pacification" than as a reflection of society's and education providers' conviction that older people's learning is important.

Unless one shares the Buddhist belief in reincarnation, learning is limited by the length of an individual lifespan. When a person dies, the unique accumulation of learning outcomes represented by that person vanishes, as far as we know, from the earth. Knowledge in one or another package may remain, but the learning represented by that individual disappears.

There should be no limits to learning other than those created by the limits of a finite lifetime. Tragically, however, fear can cause a "death" of learning potential. Little learning can occur if the learner is not free to experiment and make mistakes. When fear (justified or otherwise) blocks this freedom, the learner is diminished by the loss of a unique opportunity, and the learner's society may be commensurately impoverished. Fear can end the capacity for lifelong learning almost as certainly as death can.

Learning Is Irreversible. From Zeno's conclusion that you cannot step into the same river twice, through the relentless "moving finger" of Omar Khayyam, to Thomas Wolfe's (1940) declaration that "You can't go home again," writers and thinkers have provided testimony to the irreversibility of learning. The most powerful statement of all, perhaps, is the story of the Garden of Eden. Once a person has learned something, he or she cannot return to the world in which that thing was not known. Most outcomes of learning are positive, so the "new world" that learners are forced to enter is usually welcomed, but artistic imaginations have been stirred by situations in which the opposite was true.

Every political leader knows that the people of a country or society will not be the same tomorrow as they were yesterday. In other words, leadership must accommodate not only changes in events but changes in people. A leader can attempt to eliminate or suppress sources of learning that bring changes considered to be undesirable, but most such attempts fail, especially when the sources of learning are widespread. The Roman government attempted to suppress the learning inspired by the teachers and prophets of the Christian religion — and failed dramatically.

Learning Takes Time. Learning involves duration. You cannot be one person at one moment and another the next. Studies of apparently instantaneous, radical personal transformation, usually called conversion, indicate that it is actually the culmination of a long series of changes in the person concerned (James, 1961). Novel experiences must be considered, new responses experimented with in some sort of repetitive practice, new attitudes tested and reviewed, before these become permanent constituents of our personalities.

The amount of time needed to learn something varies greatly with the individual; one person learns quickly and with apparent ease, while another may find the same learning task lengthy and painful. The time needed for an individual's learning also may vary with the type of learning task. One person may pick up foreign languages quickly but have a "mental block" for mathematics, for example, whereas just the opposite may be true of someone else.

We accept the fact that the learning of children and young people takes time. Indeed, we have created elaborate theories and systems of education based on that assumption. We operate our schools, however, as though every student required the same length of time to learn a specified subject. As a carryover of this view, perhaps, we also seem to have organized adult society without much regard for the time that learning takes or for individual variations in that time. In the past it may have been reasonable to assume that most of life's major passages, such as from youth to adulthood, from a single state to marriage and parenthood, or from worker to supervisor, could be managed, both by the person concerned and by the society, on the basis of "built-in" opportunities to learn the new roles that occurred, more or less, at certain chronological ages. (The learning needs generated by passages will be discussed in more detail in Chapter Four.) In the complex modern world, however, in which learning is needed in so many more areas of daily life, individual differences in the time needed for learning become much more important.

Similarly, in previous periods when people married, each partner had some reason to expect that the relationship could accommodate the changes that would occur in the other as the pair passed through the various stages of maturation and aging. The divorce rate during the past forty years suggests that this expectation is no longer well founded (if it ever was). The demands for varying degrees of participation in learning, often with different outcomes, have proved too divisive for many marriages. It may be that the increasing number of families in which both partners are employed and therefore are involved in employment-related learning will be better able to assimilate the changes in individual partners than have been families in which only one partner was so engaged. There can be no doubt that in general we will have to incorporate into our social fabric more flexible allowances for the time it takes, and for differences in the time it takes, for people to learn.

Learning Cannot Be Coerced. Learning is the result of an act of will. Young people can be compelled by law to attend schools, and adults can be threatened with dire economic or other consequences if they do not acquire certain skills or attitudes, but any teacher knows that no outside force can actually compel someone to learn something. Instead of learning the subject, the coerced student merely learns to hate both subject and teacher.

An old adage that has become almost a hallmark of our commercial society states that "He who pays the piper calls the tune." This is true only if the piper already knows how to play the tune requested. If that is not the case, no amount of money in the world will produce that tune from that piper at that moment. The sponsor must allow time for the piper to learn the tune (or else seek another piper). Just as important, the piper must want to learn to play the new tune and, preferably, to learn to play it well. This will to learn — whether it is spurred by desire for money, loyalty to the sponsor, a wish to expand musical skills, or some other motivation or motivations — must come from within the piper. It cannot be imposed from outside, by money or threats or anything else.

Certain predictable loyalties grow up between learners and the sources that have stimulated their will to learn. This phenomenon is so common in educational settings that it may hardly seem worth mentioning. Almost everyone can remember an inspiring teacher who remained a treasured friend, or at least a treasured memory, long after school ended. The support, financial and otherwise, that alumni associations provide for their teaching agencies is based on loyalties of this kind.

Until recently, however, we have not paid much attention to the existence of the loyalty engendered by learning in other areas of the society, except perhaps in the armed services. Such loyalties nonetheless are clearly apparent in contemporary descriptions of large noneducational organizations with a high dependence on the successful management of learning (Peters and Waterman, 1982). Companies that provide extensive training opportunities for their employees depend on the loyalty that learning creates. The emergence of the so-called "organization man," willing to sacrifice family, private life, and even health to the good of the company, was an early example of the outcome of the provision of opportunities for learning in the business sector.

Because learning cannot be coerced, the increased dependence on lifelong learning in modern society provides a potential new dimension of freedom for the society's citizens. It also provides new challenges as leaders look for ways of supporting learning that will encourage people to want to learn.

The Distinction Between Learning and Education

The distinction between learning and education has been all but lost during the ascendancy of formal schooling in this century. A belief in not only the existence but the vital importance of this distinction, however, is central to this book and, we think, to the survival of society as well.

We can begin to approach this distinction by looking at language. The range of meanings associated with the different words for learning in the world's languages is evidence both for the importance of learning in human life and for the idea that our understanding of the meaning of learning is, to a considerable degree, culture specific. Because the meanings of words change over time, so it is desirable to subject them to fresh examination at frequent intervals. In a sense, this book is nothing more than a reexamination of the meanings of the word *learning*.

In some languages the words for "teaching" and "learn-ing" are virtually the same. This suggests a much closer identi-fication of individual and society than is assumed in English-speaking cultures, since what is taught is usually drawn from the collective knowledge and values of a society, whereas what is learned is a product of the present and past of the individual learner. To use the same word for these very different experi-ences thus implies a lack of distinction between society and in-dividual.

Few, if any, other languages have a word that achieves the inclusiveness given to the word *learning* in English. The En-glish term can be related to virtually any object or outcome. (In other languages such as French, different words are as-sociated with learning different things.) The English word *learning* can be a verb as well as a noun; that is, it can be used to represent a process or action as well as an outcome. As we have seen, this is usually the way the term is used in psychology, and it is perhaps the most common meaning of the word today, espe-cially outside the education system. In cultural, political, and sociological contexts, however, *learning* generally means an out-come of the process; that is, something that has been or will be learned. Frequently the word is used with both meanings in the same context, a confusion that is to be guarded against at all costs.

In this book we use *learning* to refer to a process. As the previous section described, that process possesses certain char-acteristics that have political, social, cultural, and economic con-sequences. We believe, as did Darwin, that our capacity for learning and for directing learning to particular objectives makes us human and that by nurturing and maximizing this capacity in ourselves, individually and collectively, we become more hu-man in the best sense of that word.

The world's languages have more consistency in the mean-ings they give to words for education. In English the word, like the noun form of *learning,* is often used to mean a sort of posses-sion, as in "She has a college education" or "We must provide a good education for the young." It also can suggest something done to someone, as in "Dr. Watson was educated at an Ivy League college." We define *education* as a complex collection of actions, procedures, and predictable results through which deliberate instruction is provided to a designated group of learners, usually called pupils or students.

Clearly education must be concerned with specific learning outcomes and with the processes of learning needed for students to achieve those outcomes. Thus education cannot exist without learning. Learning, however, not only can exist outside the context of education but probably is most frequently found there. Learning has always outstripped education, and never more so than in the present period.

Another important distinction between learning and education, in our view, is that learning is the act of an individual, whereas education is a relatively coherent group of social activities usually associated with a particular institution or institutions. Learning, in fact, is what makes human beings individual, whereas education is the institutionalized series of activities, roles, and organizations by means of which a group or society attempts to direct the learning capabilities of some or all of its members toward particular objectives. To learn is to do something by yourself. To educate is to do something to someone else.

Relationships between learning and education are so subtle that, as we have noted, the two concepts all too often have been regarded as identical. An illustration of this confusion can be seen in the numerous "aids to learning" found in college bookstores and textbook catalogues. Almost all such aids are actually designed to assist someone in learning "in school" — that is, in learning how to be taught. Few can provide assistance to learning under any other circumstances or help anyone "learn how to learn." The identification of learning with learning to be taught, and thus with education, prompts some reflection on the degree to which what has been learned is modified by the circumstances under which it was learned. Something a person has learned from being taught in school is likely to have a different meaning for that person than the "same" thing learned by means of the person's own experimentation or in the company of other people voluntarily pursuing some collective goal.

Another problem with the common confusion of learning with education is that the learning objectives associated with the major providing agencies of education (schools, colleges, and universities) have come to be accepted as the only learning objectives that are (or should be) important to either society or individual learners. The confusion between learning and education has been very much in the interest of those who provide education because of the control it gives them. We contend, however, that it is not in the best interest of society or its members.

For nearly a century we have looked to systems of education as the primary, often the only, means of dealing with the human potential for learning. We are at a point in history where that view will no longer suffice. Even if the resources available for formal education throughout the world were greatly enlarged, as educators insist that they should be, we find little evidence that any of the major problems facing our modern world would be eased or solved. We have pushed the "educational solution" as far as it will go, and we must now turn our attention to other means of nurturing, inspiring, and applying the will to learn. As the Fourth International Conference on Adult Education, sponsored by the United Nations Educational, Scientific, and Cultural Organization (UNESCO), declared (1985) we must focus not on the right to be educated but on the right to learn:

> Recognition of the right to learn is now more than ever a major challenge for humanity.
>
> The right to learn is: the right to read and write; the right to question and analyze; the right to imagine and create; the right to read one's own world and to write history; the right to have access to educational resources; the right to develop individual and collective skills.
>
> The right to learn is an indispensable tool for the survival of humanity.

In Chapter Two, we will further consider the interplay between learning and education, the growth of education as the predominant means of managing learning, the value of the development of a "learning perspective," and "Mathetics" as a distinct field of the study of learning.

2

Education:
The Social Direction
of Learning

The confusion between learning and education, and specifically the assumption that learning occurs only in the context of education, have arisen because of changes in individuals' learning needs and in society's management of learning during the past few centuries — especially in the past hundred years or so. During this time, management of learning has become both more complex and more important than ever before. The leaders of all groups to some extent, and the leaders of governments in particular, have always had to cope with and attempt to control the learning (actual and potential) of the groups' members, but the need to make intelligent decisions about that learning has never been so great. Leaders are slowly realizing that they depend on their followers' learning and need to find out more about it. They also need to make conscious decisions about who is (or ought to be) learning what, under what circumstances, by what means, at whose expense, and to what end.

Social and political change leaders manage learning by making decisions that permit, encourage, direct, or forbid the achievement of particular learning objectives. Today they must make these decisions on a scale undreamed of in earlier times. Just as the need for lifelong learning offers the greatest challenge (and opportunity) to individuals today, management of that learning offers the greatest challenge to group leaders and governments.

The way that groups and their leaders manage learning is the major concern of this book.

As the following brief history will show, the most popular form of deliberate learning management during the last century has been direction of learning through the formal educational system. (The development of this system is described in more detail in Chapter Six.) It is instructive to see how this type of learning management arose, how it became so popular as to amount to a worldwide obsession, and how and why its dominance is being challenged today.

The Mobilization of Society. The dominant characteristic of the past century throughout the world has been what Karl Deutsch (1966) called the increasing "mobilization" of populations. The mobilization of a population means more novelty in the environment of individuals in that population, resulting in an increase in both the need and the opportunity to learn. In other words, as mobilization increases, more and more people must respond constantly to new stimuli — new people, new ideas, new products, new occupations, new doctrines, and so on. Strategies of mobilization (that is, sources of constant new stimuli) include immigration, industrial development, and scientific research. The most deliberate strategy of mobilization, however, has been the provision of universal public education, with literacy as its dominant objective.

Those of us who have grown up in a modern industrial (perhaps "commercial" is a better term, since marketing is a more influential and widespread strategy of mobilization than employment) society find it hard to imagine a society in which mobilization is minimal. If our society also is made up largely of immigrants, as is true in Canada, Australia, or the United States, our imagination faces an even greater challenge. In these countries, the learning needs associated with human migration, such as the needs to cope with strange people, novel landscapes and architecture, and unfamiliar social arrangements and occupational skills, have become an accepted part of daily life, and effective responses to these challenges have become part of these societies' canons of idealized behavior. For example, the prevalence of immigration in countries such as Canada has created a policy of multiculturalism that demands tolerance of cultural differences and of the need for constant learning on a cultural level.

To people who live in a highly mobilized society, the idea of an unmobilized or minimally mobilized society may seem to be little more than a new form of the old myth of a more ordered, peaceful, and predictable past "golden age." Yet as recently as the 1940s, Viscount Haldane said at a UNESCO conference that it was enormously important to realize that the vast bulk of the world's people lived in isolated villages, working the soil as their ancestors had done before them, and never encountered a strange person or a novel idea. To understand the contrast between those people and the citizens of the industrial world of 1948, let alone the contrast between the entire world of 1948 and that of the 1990s, when few people anywhere remain in the circumstances described by Haldane, is to begin to realize the tremendous demand placed on learning today.

During most of human history, most people lived much as Haldane described them. They spent their lives in an agricultural environment that, for the most part, remained unchanged over the centuries. Skills learned in childhood from a mother, father, or village elder sufficed them for the balance of a life that probably did not last much beyond forty years. To be sure, each group of such people (tribe, village, or the like) contained a smaller group who devoted a great part of their lives to learning. These "elites" (Lasswell, Lerner, and Rothwell, 1952)— shamans or priests, hereditary or chosen secular leaders, and a limited number of others, such as artists and inventors — dealt with the outside world and were depended upon to cope with unexpected disasters such as famine, plague, or war. Only these few people came anywhere close to actualizing the human potential for lifelong learning. For most members of traditional societies, learning anything beyond the minimal skills needed for survival not only was unnecessary but often was actively discouraged.

The seeds of change in this traditional pattern were sown, in Europe at least, first by the attempt to Christianize everyone in medieval times and later by the religious strife of the fifteenth and sixteenth centuries. These seeds grew and flowered during the Industrial Revolution, which some scholars date from the invention of the mechanical printing press (Innis, [1950] 1972; McLuhan, 1969). With industrialization and the associated growth of democratic states, a new environment arose in which mobilization became the norm and lifelong learning became not only possible but necessary for the bulk of the population.

As we have seen, nothing significant happens in human affairs without some person or persons learning something that they did not know before, and such learning occurs whenever a familiar response no longer produces an expected result. This situation forces those who experience it either to learn to live with the new result or to find a new way to produce the old result. As industrialization progressed, more and more people faced such dilemmas and thus were forced to become adult learners. Most of them were not pleased with the challenge. Much of the social turbulence associated with the Industrial Revolution and the rise of democratic states can be traced to attempts to suppress or eliminate the new stimuli. Britain's machine-smashing Luddites are the most obvious example of such attempts.

Industrialization, which involves the application of complex techniques to large-scale enterprises, forced large numbers of adults to learn something new. Mining, weaving, the construction and operation of railroads, and even the keeping of small urban shops required the acquisition of novel skills or combinations of skills. Even in cases where old skills, such as digging and weaving, would suffice, people had to learn to apply these skills under new conditions. Specifically, they had to learn to work in the company of large numbers of strangers and to pace their actions by the clock.

Of all the learning outcomes imposed by the Industrial Revolution(s), these last two were perhaps the most significant. The factory system, in which large numbers of people occupied a common space, created on an unprecedented scale the most powerful of all sources of environmental ambiguity and stimuli to learning: the inescapable presence of other persons (Katz and Lazarsfeld, 1955; Tough, 1978; Kidd, 1973). In addition, "standard time," the inevitable outcome of industrialization and mechanization, produced a considerable demand for uniformity of behavior. When combined with the factory system, this standardization of time meant that all workers shared a common pattern of activity for a large part of almost every day. Ultimately it meant a standardization of individual lives that extended well beyond the workplace. Such standardization made mutual understanding across barriers of dialect, language, and culture and the learning of common attitudes and expectations much easier.

The impact of industrialization on previously intensely localized populations aided the emergence of movements for the establishment of democratic states, particularly in Western Europe and North America. These movements, like the industrialization that spawned them, required considerable learning, since they brought people into public life who had never before been thus involved. Perhaps most important, they turned subjects into citizens. *Citizen* implied a person who not only had learned the skills of public democratic behavior but was willing and able to continue his or her learning throughout a lifetime in order to take an intelligent part in the government of a nation. The supporters of democracy believed that democratic states could succeed only if every citizen was involved in such lifelong learning (Locke, 1968). Democratic states made it possible to institutionalize the potential for lifelong learning for the first time.

All these developments, particularly the combination of increasingly sophisticated work technologies and political mechanisms that required the participation of ever-larger numbers of citizens, have contributed the relentless growth of demands for more learning by more people. We are just now beginning to experience the full implications of this growth.

The Rise of the Formal Educational System. The initial impact of the demand for the learning of new skills produced by the Industrial Revolution was felt mainly by adults. As industrialization spread, however, the need for a growing, self-renewing population of industrial workers combined (often uneasily) with democratic countries' ideal of politically active citizens to produce the movement for directed learning, or education, for all children. Even though children eventually were freed from having to work in factories, their parents agreed that they must be prepared for an industrial life as well as, the parents hoped, a democratic one. The skills that these children would need could no longer be taught by parents, village elders, or even experienced craftspeople on a one-to-one or small group basis. Instead, they required inculcation by specially trained "teachers," by means of prepared programs of instruction called "curricula," in dedicated buildings referred to as "schools."

Traditionally, vocational skills had been transferred by attaching younger workers to older ones on the work site in various forms of apprenticeship. This idea is a very old one, dating back at least to medieval craft guilds and, presumably, to the manner in which children have always learned from parents and other adult relatives or neighbors. The word *apprentice* is derived from the French *apprendre,* which means "to learn." The intention of apprenticeship was that learning of a particular skill would take place with a minimum of overt teaching. The new school setting, dominated by teaching and teachers, presented a sharp contrast to this traditional way of transferring knowledge.

The idea of schools for the young has a long history in most parts of the world. Traditionally, however, such schooling was limited to the children of the elite classes. What was novel, indeed astounding, about the educational movements in the industrial societies of the late nineteenth century was their idea that *all* children should go to school, that all parents should be compelled to send their children to school, and that all adult citizens should share equally in the cost of schooling.

Since the end of the nineteenth century, these views have been adopted by every country in the world in some form or another. However, it was not until about the middle of the present century that societies began to experience the full mobilization of children by education and the effects that this produced. In Canada, for example, although compulsory school attendance laws applying to children up to at least fourteen years of age were passed by all provinces early in the century, full compliance with such laws remained little more than an ideal until the late 1930s.

The passage of child labor laws and the accessibility of urban families to the legendary truant officer made these families' participation in the educational system relatively easy to secure. Furthermore, inadequate housing, dangerous streets, and the fact that many married women worked at home made it increasingly difficult for urban families, especially the poorer ones, to supervise school-age children at home during the day. Rural families were another matter, however. Rural children, especially once they reached adolescence, remained an economic asset to their parents well into this century.

Two factors helped to bring rural children into the schools along with their urban cousins. One was the rapid decline of rural populations that began in the 1930s and continued throughout the next thirty years, until the proportion of rural to urban populations was more than reversed. The other factor, at least in Canada, was the passage in 1944 of the Family Allowance Act, which provided regular payments to all mothers of school-age children as long as those children remained in school. For the first time it became an economic advantage for poorer families in Canada, even those who had strong doubts about the usefulness of formal schooling, to support regular school attendance.

Although the tie between the Family Allowance and school attendance has been removed, a great many other structural and functional supports for school attendance by the young have come into play in Canada and elsewhere. They include declining employment opportunities for young people, the growing attraction of a youth culture that is centered on the schools, the demand for new workers' possession of more sophisticated industrial skills (which must be learned in school), the increasing movement of mothers into the labor force and the dependence of families on two incomes, and the adaptation of systems of formal education to include young people who have never been students before. (For example, the introduction in the 1960s of technical and vocational colleges in almost every province in Canada has encouraged more Canadian young people to complete secondary school and go on to college.) These supports have developed to such an extent that if all compulsory school attendance laws were erased from the books tomorrow, school attendance probably would not be affected to any appreciable degree.

Keeping more children and young people in school for longer periods of time has been the dominant goal of education during the first three-quarters of this century. At the same time, increasing numbers of objectives originally associated with learning became identified with education instead. Prevalence of the belief that learning could be directed to any and all desirable social goals through education of the young reached its zenith in the years immediately following World War II. By the end of the war, some influential American economists had reached the conclusion that the education of children and youth was the key to economic development in any culture.

It is doubtful whether any other idea has spread through the world so swiftly, been implemented on such a scale, or sprung from such high aspirations. In the twenty years between 1950 and 1970, almost every country in the world committed itself to education and spent unprecedented amounts of money to support that commitment. The high birth rate that followed World War II provided equally unparalleled numbers of children and young people to be beneficiaries of these expenditures. By the late 1960s the student population of the world, a population created and defined by education, was the largest in history.

The Growing Demand for Adult Learning. During most of this century, then, the societies of the world saw children and youth as the prime, indeed almost the sole, appropriate objects of educational endeavor. They believed that all the education — that is, all the stimulation and socialization — needed by citizens other than those of the professional class (the modern-day elites) could be provided during childhood. With the mobilization of young people by means of education contributing directly to the mobilization of succeeding generations of adults, providing for further deliberate mobilization of adult populations through education did not seem necessary. Governments and the public saw adult education as being, at best, marginal to the basic mission of educational agencies. Indeed, most people thought that it would become even more so once all children received formal education. Informal adult learning also was regarded as insignificant.

Nonetheless, since the 1950s adults have made increasing demands on educational agencies (Johnstone and Rivera, 1965; Waniewicz, 1976). These demands originated with the potential students themselves, not with educational institutions or governments. Surprisingly, the demand for access to further education came not from the failures of the elementary and secondary schools but from their successes. Information gathered from all over the world during the past forty years indicates that most adult participants in educational programs had been quite successful in their initial years of schooling. Reasons for such a pattern of participation are not difficult to guess. In most countries, educational success leads to a type of employment that makes high demands on the learning capabilities of the employee. Promotion, furthermore, may require certification of a more advanced degree of education. People who have done well in school also have acquired attitudes and habits of learning that prompt them to return to the educational system for further development.

Some societies also have had other sources of adult students. The floods of adult immigrants entering certain societies often have needed to call upon formal education to teach them, at minimum, a new language. Furthermore, as new Third World countries emerged from colonial dependence and assumed the powers of self-government, their leaders realized that they could not wait for the countries' children to grow up. They had to provide educational opportunities for their adult citizens or else the new countries would not survive.

In spite of these growing demands, most modern societies have remained relatively indifferent to the learning needs of adults. Nonetheless, governments are finally beginning to recognize the importance of adults' demand for education. Such recognition was shown, for example, in the Canadian government's consideration of the advantages of so-called skill devel-

opment leave programs for employees (Skill Development Leave
Task Force, 1983; National Advisory Panel on Skill Development Leave, 1984).

This growing recognition has come at the same time that
both governmental and public belief in the universal efficacy
of public education is declining and other vehicles for achieving learning objectives are being examined. The need for exploration of other means of managing learning arises from a
variety of factors. First, education has become a very expensive means of achieving learning objectives. It is possible that
many of the objectives now associated with education providing agencies can be accomplished for both young and old by
more economical means. Furthermore, it is now quite clear that
the education of adults should not and indeed cannot be financed
in the same way as the education of children and youth.

It also is important to note that, in spite of the growing
number of adults involved in education, more than half of the
world's population does not take part in such education, and
among that half are many adults who appear to need the type
of resources and opportunities that the formal system provides.
Research from all parts of the world is quite consistent on this
point (Waniewicz, 1976; Canadian Association for Adult Education, 1982). After thirty or more years of such reports, it is
difficult to be optimistic about the likelihood of reaching these
people by intensifying the efforts of conventional education
providing agencies. The present worldwide literacy movement
is an excellent example of using instruments for learning, as
distinct from educational agencies, as a means of reaching adults
in need of educational help. Such programs have, or could have,
broader objectives than simply increasing literacy.

Finally, the mobilization of one part of the population of
a state by means of formal education, that is, by involving that
population in the intense pursuit of particular skills and attitudes, raises profound questions about what is happening to the
rest of the population. Their lack of involvement in formal education does not mean that they are not learners (Tough, 1979;
Thomas, MacKeracher, MacNeil, and Selman, 1982). However, if what they are learning is incompatible with what the
formally mobilized segment is learning, the resulting turbu-

lence can lead to the collapse of the state of which they are a part.

The overthrow of the Shah of Iran by Muslim fundamentalists is a nearly classical example of the results of conflict between different learning objectives. The Shah and his supporters learned "the hard way" in 1979 that the bulk of the Iranian people had not been pursuing the learning objectives associated with the Shah's attempt to modernize the country. Instead, they had been attending to the lessons of Islam as taught by the exiled Ayatollah Khomeini and spread by thousands of local religious agents. The ensuing rebellion proved fatal to the Shah's government and his secular state.

Similarly, there can be little doubt that the failure of the governments of Eastern Europe, which were collapsing as this book was written, can be attributed directly to their mismanagement of learning. The economies of these countries required workers to possess increasingly sophisticated technical skills. As a result, more citizens learned more as both children and adults. The countries' political systems, however, did not evolve correspondingly to allow greater participation by these better-educated workers. The political system had to give — and it did. Attempts to compartmentalize learning for political purposes (or any others) inevitably are guaranteed to fail.

The problem of learning management is an especially acute one for democratic states that depend on some form of consensus for their survival. Their leaders must face the same questions that, left unexplored, shattered the eastern European societies: Is it possible for only part of a population to participate in lifelong learning? Can lifelong learning affect only part of the lives — for example, the part related to employment — of part of the population without affecting the rest? What resources, strategies, and protective mechanisms are needed to ensure that lifelong learning will be directed toward objectives that sustain rather than disrupt a particular society?

Toward a Learning Perspective

Practitioners of adult education over the past three decades have had the unique experience of witnessing learning in a wide variety of settings and circumstances. The skills of these practitioners, for the most part, are exercised on the grounds, both physical and intellectual, of the learners. Such circumstances present a contrast to those of the formal teacher, whose students must come to him or her, submit themselves to what is taught, and accept the decision of the teacher regarding their success or failure.

"Teaching" adults is a much more variable and mutual enterprise than teaching children and young people, particularly in formal educational settings. The teacher of adults must learn how the problem or learning need is perceived by the learners, what acceptable resources can be brought to the problem's solution, and what range of solutions is tolerable to the learners (Bryson, 1963). For example, until recently it would have been unlikely that a group of doctors trained in Western medicine would have considered herbal medications as legitimate resources or that they would have been willing to contemplate the idea that a given patient might be better off dead and therefore should be allowed or even helped to die. To persuade them to perceive such alternatives to standard medical treatment as acceptable enough to make them want to learn something about the techniques surrounding their use would have required more time, skill, and power than most educators of adults possess. In adult education, in short, the critical factors are what and how the learners are willing and able to learn rather than what the educator wants to teach.

The experience of working outside the formal symbols and practices of education has led to a growing conviction that learning is the fundamental factor in understanding not only education but all of individual and social change. It seems that learning is to education as physics is to engineering. The study of learning as both an individual and a social phenomenon is likely to be more productive in formulating basic principles of change than is the study of education.

In the early 1970s UNESCO published a report called *Learning to Be* (Faure, 1973), which described a worldwide study of education. The study had been prompted both by the unprecedented rebelliousness of students at that time and by the uneven contribution that the world's investment in education appeared to be making to economic growth. In the report the investigators stated that although they did not believe that the enormous investment in education had been a mistake, they thought the concentration of that investment solely on children and youth had been. Even more important, they said that despite the importance of formal education as an economic, political, and social instrument, it would be more productive to examine both individual and national development from the perspective of learning rather than that of education.

Even before the welcome reinforcement provided by the UNESCO report, speculation about differences between learning and education had been developing among adult educators. Allen Tough (1979) and his associates (Fair, 1973; Denys, 1973) explored the phenomenon of independent learning in a variety of settings, cultures, and adult groups. The surprise of conventional educators at these researchers' discovery of how widespread learning is and how significant it is in the lives of those investigated was ample evidence of the grip that formal systems of education had on all aspects of contemporary life. Virtually everyone apparently believed that learning (significant learning, at least) took place only in schools. It had even been suggested that, to a degree, schools caused learning.

If, as now seems clear, education is neither the only nor the best way to reach all critical learning objectives, what are the alternatives, and where shall we look for them? Research on alternative environments for learning has grown during the 1970s and 1980s (Thomas, MacKeracher, MacNeil, and Selman, 1982; Thomas, Abbey, and MacKeracher, 1983; Eurich, 1985). The principal recent development in such research has been to move from a preoccupation with individual independent learning to a focus on the characteristic ways in which organizations, including societies, manage or at least attempt to cope with their members' learning.

Those of us engaged in the exhilarating task of trying to understand the sociopolitical significance of learning and its management are trying to move beyond psychology (where the concept and most definitions of learning originated) and involve other social sciences in our work. This means persuading the professional students of these disciplines that the phenomena they grapple with are inescapably related to the learning capabilities of human beings.

So far we have found little interest among students of political science, economics, or history. In contrast, many sociologists, such as those who study work in large organizations, have been concerned with learning, although few are willing to use the word in their papers (Herzberg, 1966). The field of anthropology, too, has included solid research related to learning (Mead, 1973; Hall, 1976) and the intimate relationship between provision for learning and culture.

It is interesting to note that recent research on organizational development has begun to use the terms and methods of anthropology precisely because of the heavy involvement of many large organizations in the deliberate management of their employees' learning (Peters and Waterman, 1982). When people are encouraged to learn by their employers, larger dimensions of their lives and personalities become involved with their employment. They begin to perceive the organizations that employ them as having some characteristics of families, the traditional first source for learning. In time these organizations go on to exhibit activities usually associated with communities and cultures, such as the creation of histories, myths, and heroes. Thus the "culture" of organizations, about which we hear with increasing frequency, grows out of those organizations' management of learning.

Drawing together information and researchers from various social sciences is the beginning of an attempt to create a new field of study devoted to learning. The UNESCO report, which recommended the development of such a field, suggested that it should be called Mathetics (from the Greek word meaning "to learn"). The field would include a combination of our understanding of learning as a psychological phenomenon and our recognition of the manifestations of learning as phenomena of social, economic, historical, political, and moral importance.

A renewed focus on learning rather than education and a recognition of the importance of learning in all human activities can lead to a "learning perspective" from which any society can be studied and evaluated. We will explain this perspective in more detail and provide a matrix for applying it systematically in Chapter Seven. Basically, this perspective requires understanding that learning is the prime dynamic of contemporary society, particularly of the economy, and that most political decisions are really decisions about the management of learning. This perspective will reveal that there are many means besides educational ones of reaching learning objectives and that formal education can handle only a part of the learning that our society both demands and stimulates.

In the next chapter we will advance a different kind of theoretical framework or schema for describing the dynamics of learning in a society. It divides the life of a society into three domains: the Social Domain, the Learning Domain, and the Educational Domain. The chapter will describe the distinctive characteristics of each domain and show the nature and significance of the roles that each requires people within it to play.

3 ❧

Understanding
the Social Dynamics
of Learning

Dealing with learning, as opposed to dealing with education, requires us to consider all of the complex web of activities that compose a society and to examine them from the perspective of both individuals and groups. (We use *society* as a sort of umbrella term; our analysis can apply to human groups of any size.) Individual learners must make decisions about both the process and the outcomes of their learning. Societies or other groups also must make decisions in order to cope with the fact that their members can and do learn.

The nature of individual and collective decisions about the management of learning is determined by time, culture, geography, accident, and other specific circumstances. For example, a fourteenth-century European noble might decide to send his teenage son to the court of a neighboring noble so that the son could learn the arts and skills of warfare and of managing a large estate. The noble's daughter might be sent to a convent to learn the arts and skills of domestic life. The noble himself might decide that a pilgrimage to Rome would aid his spiritual and temporal development.

A contemporary American working-class family would have very different but equally important learning decisions to make. Such a family is obliged by law to send its children to school. That schooling may result in the opportunity to enter a college or university, with the expectation that this advanced education will result in greater income and occupational satisfaction. Alternatively, the children of such a family might follow their initial schooling with some sort of vocational training, publicly or privately provided, which would lead more quickly to employment. Both parents in the family, being employed, may be union members and may decide to enroll in educational programs made available by their unions. Instead, they may decide to take advantage of training programs given by their employers that offer a path to promotion or more interesting work.

However various the decisions about learning might be, we believe that they have certain features in common. Figure 1, which we have called the Learning Map, shows the three "domains" among which people can move by making decisions about the management of learning. We have named these domains the Social Domain, the Learning Domain, and the Educational Domain. Individual decisions are shown by the top diagonal line. At point A, a person exists in the realm of everyday needs, the Social Domain, and makes decisions in an attempt to meet those needs. When the person recognizes that one or more of these needs must be translated into learning needs, the person moves into the Learning Domain and makes decisions that attempt to meet these learning needs (B). A decision to turn a learning need into an educational need moves the person into the Educational Domain, where he or she will have to make decisions about educational needs (C).

The bottom diagonal line represents group decisions, including political decisions. Decisions about what everyday needs will be met and how, and about which of these needs will be regarded as learning needs, take place in the Social Domain at point A1. Which learning needs will be met and how, and whether they will be translated into educational needs, are the collective decisions made in the Learning Domain (point B1). Collective decisions in the Educational Domain (C1) concern which and whose educational needs will be met and by what means.

The map inevitably is limited in that it suggests that the

Figure 1. The Learning Map.

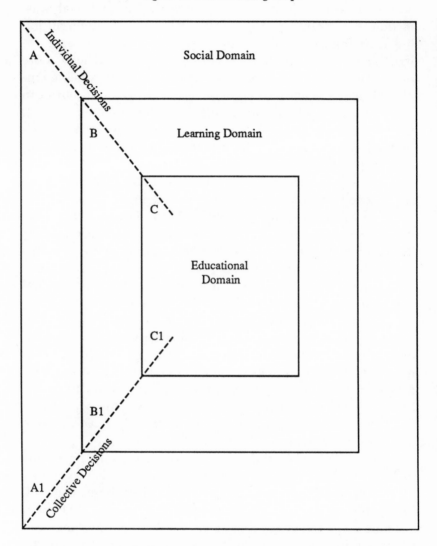

path of these decisions is much more linear, unidirectional, and static than is really the case. Individuals and groups actually act simultaneously in all three domains and shift their activities from one to another in any order. For example, control of the learning necessitated by the AIDS epidemic has been shifted from the Learning Domain to the Educational Domain, and we are presently witnessing attempts to shift that control to the Social Domain, where instruments of the legal system can be applied to it. When AIDS was thought to be associated with a relatively small group, homosexual men, the response to the learning needs created by the illness was to persuade those involved to learn how to avoid the disease. As the threat became more general, attention shifted to using mass media and the educational system in an attempt to alter the behavior of the entire population. Most recently, legal steps have been taken to compel identification of victims and the testing of various segments of the population. The movement from the Learning to the Educational Domain and then to the legal instruments of the Social Domain is typical of societal decisions about the management of learning.

The rest of this chapter will examine the individual decisions and activities that characterize each of the three domains in more detail. It will also describe the principal roles that people assume when taking part in each domain. Chapters Five and Six will discuss the collective decisions in each domain that are made necessary by the learning occasions described in Chapter Four.

The Social Domain

People's daily life is conducted primarily in the Social Domain. A person's activities in this domain are devoted to attempting to satisfy his or her various needs. Hunters hunt, farmers cultivate the soil, industrial workers attend to their machines in order to provide food, clothing, shelter, and other necessities and comforts for themselves and perhaps their families. Needs for physical and psychological security are met by forming various groups, which compete with other groups for access to and control of land and other resources. In the past, groups established for political purposes have assumed such forms as tribe, kingdom, empire, and commune; today they are usually nation-states.

Within these larger and more complex groups or states,

smaller groups compete in deciding (or trying to affect others' decisions) about which needs are most important and how those needs should be met. Such competition is not the only activity in the Social Domain, but it is a very important one. It extends from demands for self-determination by ethnic groups in India, Sri Lanka, and the Soviet Union to the now-legendary conflict between sheep and cattle ranchers in the American West and current rivalries for control of sources of electric power and water. Such rivalries are an unavoidable part of the fabric of social life. The measure of all statecraft is its success or failure in maintaining some degree of order in the expression of these rivalries and in curbing people's tendency to believe that the solution to them lies in removing competing claims by killing those claims' supporters.

The most inclusive role associated with the Social Domain is that of citizen. Theoretically this role includes all others, such as the economic roles of entrepreneur or worker; the social roles of parent, sibling, and friend; and the political roles of government leader or elected representative, to name but a few. Whatever else people are, they are all citizens of some state and have at least the potential to take an active part in that state's government.

In many societies, children have been excluded from full participation in the Social Domain on the grounds that they should not and could not be expected to determine and pursue all their own needs until they had learned sufficient skills and acquired sufficient maturity to do so effectively. The children of hunting and farming societies acquired responsibility as full members of those societies very much earlier than the children of contemporary industrial societies, however. What the former needed to learn was much less complex, and the means of learning were more easily combined with adult pursuits. Industrial societies have been increasingly characterized by the exclusion of children from the citizen role for long periods of time. In such societies it is considered proper that children be preoccupied exclusively with the learner role of the Learning Domain and, increasingly, with the student role of the Educational Domain.

The Learning Domain

As we explained in Chapter Two, changes in the environment often cause a formerly successful method of meeting a need to fail. When this happens, a person may translate the unmet need in the Social Domain into a need for learning—that is, for seeking new behavior that will meet the original need. If the person decides to try to satisfy that learning need, he or she enters the Learning Domain (the rectangle just inside the Social Domain in Figure 1). To be sure, the person most likely continues to function in the Social Domain as well, especially if the person is an adult. Indeed, increasing numbers of adults are choosing to juggle simultaneous roles in all three domains (Tough, 1979; Hiemstra, 1979; Brookfield, 1984).

The learning outcomes sought in the Learning Domain are of two basic kinds. The first is the highly visible, dramatic learning associated with discovery, invention, and research: learning what no one has ever known before. Artists and craftspeople seek this outcome just as much as do scientists and engineers. Successful learning of what no one has ever known requires freedom to imagine possibilities and to make mistakes without dooming the learner or the learning enterprise. Unfortunately, this freedom has been limited dramatically in the past twenty years by the increasing institutionalization of research in both industry and academia. The contrast between the relaxed disorder of Edison's Menlo Park and the discipline of the modern industrial or university laboratory is powerful evidence of the continuing social attempt to "capture" this form of learning.

The second major type of learning outcome occurs when a person learns something that he or she did not know before, although other people have known it. Achievement of this kind of outcome also requires freedom to imagine and experiment, though perhaps to a less intense degree than the other kind. This second kind of outcome can create just as earthshaking a change in the person involved as the first kind. It usually has much less dramatic social effects, but not always. For example, the Workers' Education Association, which was formed in Great Britain in the early 1900s, brought British workers with little formal education into "informal" contact with the liberal studies of British universities (Joint Committee of University and Work, 1909). This meant that British working men learned what British middle class, mostly young, men had been learning for more than a century — but they learned it from a very different background of experience. The results of this confrontation between different points of view was impressive for both learners and instructors, as old lessons took on new meanings (Fieldhouse, 1977). One effect of the program could be seen in the fact that almost every member of the cabinet of the Labour Government elected in 1945 proved to have been either a student or an instructor in the Workers' Education Association.

The Role of Learner. The primary role in the Learning Domain is that of learner. The initial decisions associated with the learner role, as described by Allen Tough (1979) and his students (Fair, 1973; Denys, 1973), are as follows:

- identification of what needs to be learned (usually a provisional act, since objectives frequently change during the learning process);
- determination of how it is to be learned (that is, what appropriate resources for learning are available and how they are to be approached);
- establishment of how much the learning endeavor(s) will cost (or, perhaps more important, how much the learner is willing to pay);
- calculation of the amount of time likely to be involved in the learning process (probably a compromise between the amount of time needed for ideally complete learning and the amount of time that the learner has available) and the distribution of that time (a small amount each day or week for an extended period, or a solid block of time such as a two-week vacation);
- determination of the point at which the project either will be held to be complete — that is, the learning objective will have been achieved to the learner's satisfaction — or will be

abandoned as being impossible to carry out, at least in its original terms. (This last decision marks the single unalterable distinction between the Learning Domain and the Educational Domain in that the decision is made by the learner in the Learning Domain but is made by the education provider in the Educational Domain.)

A practical example may make the nature of these decisions clearer. Suppose a person who has never done so before decides to build a garage. The person might first consult sources of home improvement information to get some idea of the scope of the project and the kinds of skills and knowledge that it would require. The person might also try to find and talk with someone who has actually built a garage. He or she might ask friends for advice and perhaps help as well. The person probably will also query suppliers about materials, equipment, prices, the technical aspects of using one type of design rather than another, and so on. (Small businesses are underappreciated learning resources.) He or she finally will decide on the materials and design to be used and the amount of money that can be allotted for supplies and will determine to build the garage during, say, an upcoming three weeks of vacation time.

Construction of the garage eventually begins. Our do-it-yourselfer most likely encounters unexpected difficulties, tries out and discards ideas, and seeks the help of friends and suppliers in solving special problems such as "pitching" the roof. At last, with luck and persistence, the building is completed — not quite as it had been envisioned, perhaps, but completed to a reasonable level of satisfaction. The experience may lead the person to vow never to undertake such a project again or even to conclude that this one never should have been undertaken in the first place. At the other extreme of possibility, it may make him or her decide to start a construction business. Whatever the outcome, the project *has* been undertaken, and it can never be undertaken by that person in exactly the same way again. Both the completed structure and the results of the learning involved in completing it are now part of this brave individual's resources.

Activities and procedures in the Learning Domain are often compared with those in the Educational Domain, and we will do so later in this chapter. However, they can be compared with the activities in the Social Domain as well. In the Social Domain, too, objectives are identified and skills are called into action. In this domain, however, these skills are already known to the person using them, so putting them to work requires little conscious thought or expenditure of time. The overall purpose of the action is not to learn something new but to bring about a desired result. In fact there is often resistance to learning in the Social Domain, arising in part from a wish that life, friends, and self should remain dependably familiar and predictable.

In contrast, the process of learning (and the role of being a learner), as we showed in Chapter One, requires both time and attention. Before we can make the new response we would like to make, we must direct a considerable amount of effort and time to pursuing the steps required to achieve that response. Furthermore, the process is never simply one of adding responses; we must incorporate the new responses into our existing repertoire, which means that everything we are must alter to some degree. Sometimes this involves "unlearning" or discarding responses that have met needs in the past but now fail to do so. Anyone who has undertaken professional athletic training after having already achieved a modest degree of proficiency in the sport in question knows the pain and determination involved in eliminating or altering existing responses.

A profound act of surrender to the objective and the procedures chosen to attain it also is required. We have to make this surrender because we cannot guarantee that we will achieve our ultimate goal, only that we will follow the procedures believed to lead to it, and we cannot know who or what we will be if we do achieve it. Being a learner involves an element of vulnerability because of the possibility of making a mistake and needing to retrace one's steps. There is always a moment, mostly fleeting but sometimes, in the case of major transformations, lasting for a seeming eternity, in which we are open, exposed, and torn by the conflict of past and future selves.

The Role of Group Member. Participation in groups can provide a powerful stimulus for learning and the identification of learning needs, even though learning itself can be carried out only by individuals. This stimulus comes not only from the intense stimulation provided by other people, each of whom necessitates trying out a novel set of responses until some form of familiar relationship is developed, but also the stimulation resulting from the demands of group objectives, which require skills and knowledge to accomplish. The secondary role in the Learning Domain, therefore, is that of group member. Far more learning probably is accomplished in this role than in the role of student, the key role of the Education Domain.

The most basic group that requires learning of its members is the family. World literature is full of accounts of the learning that takes place within the family ("coming of age" stories, for example) and of successful and unsuccessful attempts by families to cope with the learning of their child or adult members. Beyond the family are countless groups, formal or informal, to which a learner might belong, including groups of coworkers in a place of employment, professional groups, and a wide variety of voluntary groups. All of these groups can stimulate learning in many ways.

In some societies, volunteer groups automatically are regarded as possible threats to order and the state. Indeed, some of these groups truly present such threats because of what their members learn and display as possible alternatives to the learning objectives allowed or supported by the state. In liberal democratic states, however, the freedom to associate publicly and privately usually is not limited unless it can be demonstrated that such association is treasonable or seditious. From this freedom comes substantial learning. Indeed, it is precisely because people (both children and adults) learn so much of such great importance to themselves and society from other people that freedom of association is so important to human life.

Where such freedom exists, the "market" of competing models of behavior and ways of satisfying needs provides more stimulus for more learning by more people than any other source. The scope and complexity of this informal "learning market" has increased steadily in recent years as more independent organizations, including trade unions, development associations, cultural organizations, and groups concerned with the preservation of health or the environment, have provided vehicles through which individuals can take larger roles in public life. It is no accident that the procedures engaged in by individual learners in pursuing individual and collective goals are so similar to the procedures required of the ordinary citizen of the democratic state as envisioned by its founders. These wise men seem to have understood that democratic citizenship and lifelong participation in learning were in fact the same goal.

Yet this freedom is always in danger. Learning cannot be coerced, but it can, for short periods of time, be co-opted (Ellul, 1967; Hale, 1964). The objectives of organized groups can be distorted or misdirected by unscrupulous leaders, particularly when it is a large group. The organizational structure of the Teamsters' Union allowed James Hoffa to misdirect its objectives, for example, even though many ordinary members continued to contribute their learning potential to the union. Similarly, voluntary organizations in Nazi Germany were not all destroyed or sent underground; most were simply captured. Perhaps precisely because the freedom to learn is fragile and not always consciously recognized, it presents a constant temptation to those who want to weaken it through orchestrated enthusiasms and fraudulent participation.

The existence of educational institutions is not necessarily a guarantee of this freedom, since they frequently present even easier targets for the manipulator or the demagogue than do voluntary groups. Worse still, they have recently seduced themselves into believing that the directed learning they represent is the only learning that is important. Still, learners usually cannot be tricked twice, and although learning can be perverted for brief periods of time, it cannot be entirely suppressed even through killing or exile. It is in the roles and procedures of the Learning Domain that some of the most profound manifestations not only of learning itself but of democratic life and individual freedom can be found.

The Educational Domain

Citizens of societies sophisticated enough to provide systems of formal education may choose to translate some of their learning needs into educational needs. An educational need is one that can be satisfied only by resorting to some part of an educational system, the primary business of which is teaching. In the terms of our Learning Map, a person must enter the Educational Domain in order to satisfy an educational need.

Some observers have argued that all formal education is "education at a distance," a term currently used only to describe educational agencies' increasing use of media such as telephone, radio, and television to carry their programs beyond their traditional precincts. Until the rise of the school on a large scale during and after the Industrial Revolution, learning had been accomplished primarily at home, among family and neighbors who found it relatively easy to combine the nourishment of learning in the young with the pursuit of satisfaction of adult needs. With the development of formal schooling, however, children were removed from this inclusive environment and subjected to deliberate instruction aimed at satisfying both the present and future needs of the families from which they came and the needs of their community and nation. Therefore, the first "learning at a distance" involved the distance, both physical and psychological, between the Learning and the Educational domains. That distance still exists, and it has important implications not just for the young but for everyone.

Reasons for Entering the Educational Domain. At times a person may move directly from the Social Domain to the Educational Domain without having consciously translated a learning need into an educational need. This happens most obviously in the case of children forced by law to attend school. For adults and older youths it is most likely to happen when large and highly visible educational agencies are persuasive in their claims to control all significant learning, thus causing people to think that they have to enter the educational system in order to learn. It also can happen when a supportive public (such as existed in America in the 1950s and 1960s) believes that education is the cure for all difficulties, particularly economic ones, and therefore persuades large numbers of people to seek further education. The clamorous "stay in school" campaign of the 1960s in Canada, in which community pressure on a large scale was directed at persuading seventeen- and eighteen-year-olds to complete their secondary schooling as a means of ensuring later employment, was an example of that public temper. Present evidence suggests that the argument was erroneous, even foolish, but it took a decade to discover that fact.

Besides law, the attraction of a visible and accessible educational system, and public pressure, there are at least four other reasons for deciding to enter the Educational Domain. One is a need for reassurance, for legitimacy. As we have mentioned, learning—the deliberate transformation of oneself—can be a lonely affair. In addition to quite possibly being divided from within (the potential new self in conflict with the old), the learner is also apt to be isolated from without, since friends and loved ones may be disturbed or even alienated by the emerging "new person." (George Bernard Shaw observed that despite all the sadness associated with the death of a loved one, there was also a tiny amount of satisfaction that that person was now complete and could be "tidied up"; one would never again have to be bothered by having to adjust to unpredictable learning by that person.)

Sometimes a learner can gain support for new learning from membership in a group, but by no means always. Studies of groups in which intense learning occurs (Homans, 1950) emphasize the need for such groups to maintain themselves by reassuring each member that he or she is safe, cherished, and capable of persevering and achieving the desired changes. Such support often is not forthcoming, however, because by learning we shake the confidence of those around us in our predictability. Records of adult learning are full of stories of peers applying pressure to discourage attempts by individuals to learn and thereby change themselves.

It is no surprise, then, that doubt about both the means and the ends of learning frequently assails the learner, and the spirit flags. An educational agency, however, legitimizes both ends and means in the eyes of the student, family, and friends. Reassurance is provided by the very authority of the agency and by the fact that so many others have accepted, even welcomed, that authority. Friends and loved ones often make a special allowance for the disturbances and turbulence that may result from formal study, although those allowances are likely to be somewhat less generous for older students.

A somewhat related reason for entering an educational agency is to seek the benefits of membership in a group that is undertaking learning tasks similar to one's own. We have pointed out the overriding importance of group membership in the life of the independent learner. The proof of that significance is demonstrated by the degree to which educational agencies at all levels seek to create a sense of membership in an environment that is fundamentally individual in character. Grades and degrees, diplomas and certificates, are given only to individuals. But although the ends of education are individual, just like the ends of learning, the means, with few exceptions, are collective, and much effort is expended to maximize the contribution of membership to learning within educational boundaries. From the "bluebirds" and "swallows" into which elementary classes are often subdivided to team sports and the debating, stamp, music, and science clubs of high school and college and the mythical "community of scholars" in the university, the attempt to harness the dynamics of group life to the pursuit of individual educational goals is evident.

This emphasis on group membership offers some clues to the reason for the apparent indifference that educational agencies accord to part-time students: No matter how good their grades or how assiduous their study habits, these students are not perceived by teachers or administrators as being true members of the student community (Boyer, 1987). It is assumed, often correctly, that the conditions of their participation (little time on campus, and that most commonly at night, coupled with the demands of jobs, family, and other responsibilities of adult citizens) will not permit such membership. Since most of the practices of educational agencies are designed to support the educational "community" and its full-time members, a downward spiral results in which the part-time student's difficulties in participating in an institution's group life are exacerbated by prevailing administrative arrangements.

One major effect of the radical student protests of the 1960s was the restoration of some sense of true community to the huge, impersonal, isolating organizations that sheer force of student numbers had caused teaching agencies to become. Students brought about this sense of community by creating their own groups within the universities and by insisting on student participation in the government of the universities and, to a lesser extent, in secondary and other postsecondary schools.

Nevertheless, the quality of learning associated with membership can never be entirely recreated within teaching agencies, no matter how hard they or their students may try, because their final goal is not group but individual achievement and because the participants in educational groups have only limited freedom in their choice of associates. Students' inclusion in classes is directed by the educational authorities, and the extracurricular groups open to them are open only to other students and must be approved by those same authorities. Groups established inside the educational system represent an attempt to replicate the Learning Domain within the Educational Domain — an attempt that is at best only moderately successful.

Educational agencies also both provide and legitimize substantial resources. Teachers, laboratories, equipment, books, libraries, all exist for no other purpose than providing instruction for the student. Even the part-time learner, whose access to supporting facilities is often limited, is surrounded by an ambience that supports the determination to be a student and the comforting presence of peers engaged in similar activities.

The final reason for a decision to enter the Educational Domain is the most obvious: teaching agencies have the exclusive power to certify the achievements of their students. The primacy of this function is attested to by the many "nontraditional" educational experiments undertaken by teaching agencies in the 1960s and 1970s (Gould, 1974). In all of those experiments, which were largely designed to modify the dimensions of the student role, the one function that remained unaltered was that of the evaluation and subsequent certification of the student's achievements by the teaching agency.

Bound up as it is with the protection of the public, we can easily understand why tampering with this function endangers the entire agency and even, perhaps, the society to some extent. The achievements of self-managed learning usually are known to and recognized by only the learner and perhaps his or her friends and family. Often this may be enough, but it is unlikely to suffice if the learner's aim is to market these achievements publicly, in seeking employment for example. Therefore the learner turns to the agency, which, at a price (financial and otherwise), is willing and able to give a public stamp of approval (certification) to his or her learning achievements. More and more often such certification is not only a help but a requirement in seeking employment or advancement.

The Student Role. In order to satisfy an educational need, a person must take on the dominant role of the Educational Domain, that of student. The word *student* is used here because it universally seems to represent the educational role associated with older youth and adults. Children are more usually called *pupils.* The precise moment when one shifts from the role of pupil to that of student is unclear in most countries, but in North America it is generally associated with entrance to secondary school. In countries like Finland, however, loyalty to classical language prevails and the word *pupil* is used formally into the university years. *In pupilari* was the classical phrase for people subject to control, discipline, and instruction. "Student" has a history of greater independence, as in the *studium generale* of the thirteenth century. Increasingly the more self-enhancing word *student* has become entrenched, but in reality there may not be much difference between the roles of student and pupil. Perhaps the most significant fact about the student/pupil role is that it is created and maintained by educational systems. Without teaching of some kind, there can be neither students nor pupils.

Until recently the student role was perceived to involve only children (pupils), youth, and a small number of older people who were either pursuing "higher" (postsecondary) educational objectives or taking remedial courses to make up for lost educational opportunities. The education of this latter group was regarded as a privilege dispensed, for the most part somewhat grudgingly, by educational providers, and the group's particular needs played little or no part in the plans or procedures of the providing agencies. When "students" were referred to in public, these adults were not included. Today, however, the radical increase in the numbers of adult students at all levels of education in many countries has forced a new perception of what the word *student* means.

The main distinction between pupil and student lies in the fact that the vast majority of students pursue their studies voluntarily, whereas pupils usually are compelled by law to participate in education. This argument suggests that *student* is a more specialized and precisely defined form of *learner,* since learners also pursue their objectives voluntarily. This is true to some extent, but the processes and outcomes of learning associated with the student role are subject to identifiable and predictable opportunities and limits, whereas those of the learner are not.

The role of student has a lengthy history. It can be classed as a semipublic role, in contrast to the role of learner, which remains essentially private. The semipublic nature of the student role began in Europe in the eleventh and twelfth centuries, where, for the first time, learners clustered together to create the beginnings of universities (Rashdall, 1936; Waddell, 1927, 1933). To be sure, there had been students in Greece and Rome and schools with pupils earlier than that, but the prevailing Western image of the student found its origins in Bologna, Padua, Paris, and later in most European cities of any size. The institutionalized "in loco parentis" college style, with its more restrained student (typified by the students of Oxford and Cambridge), appeared at a slightly later date.

Critical, restless, frequently insolent, students have always enjoyed some degree of public immunity. In some periods, such as the present, students have been exempted from paying certain fees and taxes and sometimes from having to perform military service. In others, universities were outside of civic control entirely. This protection has not been limited to the Western world. In the Middle East and Asia, even before the influx of Western models, students and the scholars to whom they were apprenticed enjoyed special status and immunity from some ordinary adult responsibilities. Generally such privileges have been granted partly because of the students' youth, partly because of their numbers, and partly because of their apparent promise for achieving the overall betterment of society.

It was only after the middle of this century, when the number of students grew so large, that some unexpected implications of these privileges became painfully apparent. Governments, as well as many average citizens, found it difficult, if not impossible, to tolerate the presence of thousands of rebellious young men and women lecturing the public on how to conduct their lives while living principally at the expense of that same public. Discontent increased when these students emerged from their privileged "ivory towers" to interfere directly with public business, giving a new and frequently bloody (on both sides) definition to traditional conflicts between town and gown. This happened in many American universities and among the students of Paris in the 1960s and more recently in Korea, Burma, and China as well.

It is doubtful whether Western countries will ever witness such turbulent events again, except perhaps in some small and particularly isolated postsecondary institutions. The decline in size of the age groups from which these rebellious students came, combined with the recent rise in the age of full-time students (bringing with it the likelihood of greater maturity and more ties to the community), suggests that the role of student is undergoing a major change. It is clear that few, if any, states can afford to extend unchanged to large numbers of older students the financial and other privileges that they have previously offered to young ones.

Patterns of Student Life. Student life, like the life of all learners, is focused on the future. It is a life of effort, determination, and hope, aimed at the achievement of some specified proficiency and some unspecified understanding that will allow a person to do and be what he or she desires. The distinction between student and learner is that for the student, most of the components of that life are externally controlled.

Even more than adult work life, student life is dominated by time. However much the exact intervals involved may differ (for example, in equatorial countries the school day is usually 7 A.M. to 1 P.M.), the time patterns of educational systems are remarkably similar throughout the world. All feature fixed bursts of activity, regular intermissions, and repetition.

At the lower levels of the system it appears that many of these arrangements are less related to the nature of learning than to social necessities. In earlier times these necessities included the requirements of agricultural life (need for children's help on the farm during especially busy times), the need to celebrate religious holidays, and so on. Today most of the necessities arise from the growing number of families in which both parents are employed outside the home. Such families have become almost totally dependent upon school systems to occupy and supervise their children for most of every day and most of every year, at no greater expense than the payment of regular taxes. As higher levels of education are reached, the time scheme more nearly reflects the demands of learning (students in college and to some extent in secondary school can choose how many courses to take, for example). Nonetheless, the determination of the way that time will be spent for the most part remains outside of student control.

Student life is divided into discrete segments of time: class hours, terms, semesters, years. For the most part, the material presented during these fixed time periods is determined by teachers' decisions about how long an average group of students should take to master particular subject matter. Little allowance is made for individual differences in the time needed for learning. The material is adapted to fit the preordained time periods, and individual students are expected to adapt to fit the material.

In the early stages of schooling, the year is the time period that predominates. Each grade or form is defined by the "school year," which varies in length and location in the calendar from country to country but generally lasts nine to ten months. The school year dominates the calendar year, particularly the rhythm of family life, because the school day partly determines the family day.

A good example of the power of education as an institution and its control of the school year was exhibited in the province of Ontario in the mid-1960s. Because the period from January to Easter, which normally occurs in April, seemed interminable to teachers and pupils alike, the government, the principal educational authority in the province, decided to interrupt that long period with a midwinter break of one week's duration and reduce the length of the holiday (traditionally Easter) that comes at the end of the term. As well as creating a bonanza for the tourist and amusement industries, this decision had the effect of transforming Easter from a major holiday into a minor long weekend. Control of time is the ultimate power, and this decision demonstrated the degree to which such control had shifted from the church (whose bells were once Western society's main timekeepers) to the school.

Some of the time units in the educational system were dictated originally by the pattern of life in the external society. In North America, for example, the predominance of an agricultural way of life made it necessary for all but the smallest pupils to be available for work during spring planting and the harvest season. The result was the lengthy "summer vacation" that is so important to present North American society.

Agriculture is no longer the occupation of most North Americans, but summer vacation persists. To be sure, a variety of educational activities has invaded the summer months, but their character tends to be different from that of activities carried out during the regular academic year. (They focus more on the arts, for example.) Even when "summer school" does teach regular program material, summer classes tend to be both experienced and evaluated somewhat differently than similar classes held from September to December and January to April. Often they are remedial classes.

Now that summer vacation is no longer needed for farm labor, many students use it to earn income to pay for their education during the rest of the year. This practice, which has allowed families with limited incomes to send their children to college and university in larger numbers than otherwise would have been possible, was seriously disrupted during the 1960s and 1970s by an abnormally large number of students seeking jobs combined with a decrease in the relatively unskilled jobs that traditionally had been available to them.

In Canada, the government intervened in 1970 with a special program, entitled "Opportunities for Youth," that was intended to replace vanishing sources of student income. The program provided money to groups of students who advanced acceptable proposals for activities to be undertaken by members of the group. Such projects included provision of community services for deprived people and sometimes creation of local action groups. The government thus provided the students with chances to engage in the more powerful learning opportunities characteristic of the Learning Domain, as distinct from those of the Educational Domain. Regrettably, no thorough evaluation of this program exists, but it was a creditable, if frequently contentious, exercise in the support of learning and (indirectly) of citizenship. There is little doubt that students who had been involved in the program returned to their formal studies transformed by new and unique experiences as learners. Furthermore, the principle involved in this program, of support for the initiative of small groups of citizens, found its way into other programs of the decades, although only one of these (a program called New Horizons, which supports similar projects designed and carried out by citizens over the age of 65) still exists.

A second important pattern of student life has to do with its physical circumstances. With few exceptions, students must travel to the school. From the one-room schoolhouse of early North America to the five- and six-story lycees and gymnasiums of Europe and the often highly dispersed universities and colleges in cities throughout the world, schools are detached, segregated, single-purpose buildings. They are designed for the instruction of students and, with the possible exception of research facilities in universities, for nothing else.

The necessity for schools to be separate, both physically and psychologically, from the "real world" arises from one of the major characteristics of learning, the need for the freedom to experiment (with both materials and ideas) and make mistakes without suffering the consequences that might be suffered in the external world. All teaching agencies set limits to permissible student behavior, but (theoretically at least) they are much more flexible than the world outside.

The separation of teaching agencies from the rest of society enormously enhances students' sense that the school belongs to them exclusively and should have their nurture and support as its sole responsibility. This cloistered freedom has a price, however. It appears both in the student's feeling of being isolated physically and intellectually from the outside world and in the problems that the student often encounters when, following the completion of a program of studies, he or she returns to that world. As student bodies grow older and become composed of more people with stronger ties to the community than is typical of the unmarried, newly independent young, and as the numbers of part-time students (with their minimal involvement in or commitment to the social aspects of student life) increase, this protective segregation may be severely eroded. The effect of this loss is unknown, but there is no doubt that it will be profound. One possible way of maintaining some of this protection of students might be the reestablishment of the apprenticeship relationship characteristic of the research-based universities that emerged in Germany and elsewhere in the nineteenth century, which seems to be happening in some of the new postgraduate research institutions.

The physical and psychological segregation of formal education allows for, indeed necessitates, the creation and maintenance of complex societies within teaching agencies. As we have seen, the existence of these internal societies enhances the feeling of "membership" substantially, even though participating in them is sometimes compulsory. Any outsider who contemplates a school notice board is forcibly reminded of the exclusiveness of the society that it reflects. Alumni associations and the loyalties that sustain them arise out of these enclosed societies.

These same circumstances provide impressive obstacles to those who must or wish to study on some basis other than that of the full-time, "residential" student. Part-time studentship has worked for many, but in most societies there are even more individuals who are intellectually able to pursue courses of study but cannot make themselves available at any conventional times (Perry, 1977). These people's demand for access to the educational system has increased commensurately with the general increase in the number of adult students and has resulted in considerable experimentation with the student role. The Open University in Britain (Lewis, 1983) has been the most impressively successful of these experiments, and it now has many counterparts throughout the world. Much attention was directed to the Open University's use of instructional devices, but the true basis of its success was the provision of local support groups, tutors, and summer school. It identified a sizable population of academically able learners who for various reasons could not afford to take up the conventional role of student. In addition, the introduction of new technology in communications and information processing (computers, video, and so on) has brought rapid development in what has come to be known as "education at a distance" (Kegan, 1986; Mugridge and Kaufman, 1986). All these experiments, most notably the Open University, have demonstrated the absolute necessity of maintaining some form of membership experience among the students of a particular agency, no matter how widely scattered they may be.

The life of a student, even a full-time one, tends to focus on short-term relationships. The relatively prolonged relationship with a single teacher that is characteristic of schools for small children is abandoned fairly early in most systems in favor of an organizational arrangement that allows a wide variety of people to present to students their specialized knowledge. From secondary school upwards in most systems, students must choose not only different courses but different instructors, with each of whom their contact is likely to be relatively short.

Similar conditions apply to relationships with other students, since each program or class involves a different student group. Small groups of students may cling together while they climb the educational ladder, as often happens in professional schools, but teaching agencies take no account of that in their planning. The rapid social changes entailed by student life in fact may be more suitable to older students, who are less likely to need social supports in the school setting than do the younger ones. However, this atomization may intensify in the future and may have unexpected effects on the quality of life in educational agencies and on the outcomes of their work.

Finally, student life is a life of procedures: fulfilling requirements, attending classes, completing assignments, taking examinations, meeting deadlines. These activities demand a relatively limited repertoire of skills—listening, reading, writing, speaking, calculating—although the activities also are presumed to develop more complex abilities of thinking, reasoning, and feeling. As students advance, they are encouraged to specialize, which further narrows the range of skills demanded. These skills may not be the same ones required for coping with the outside society, in which, for example, the transfer of information is less and less dominated by print.

Every teaching agency has its own biases about the nature of knowledge and the best means of pursuing it. These biases will appear most clearly, not in the instructional material that the agency presents, but in the procedures and means of instruction it chooses. There is no way to avoid such biases, but it is incumbent on any society to review from time to time what these biases are and determine what modification or correction they may need.

Limitations of the Student Role. The "form" in formal education is found in the student role and the patterns of student life. Public attention tends to focus on the content of education, but the rites and rituals of student life actually are more profoundly influential and more thoroughly learned. "Psyching out the system," or learning how these patterns work, has always been the great game of students.

Work with adults who have returned to formal education after even a brief absence indicates clearly that such people face a double challenge, that of mastering the subject matter and that of learning how to be students again (Thomas and Klaiman, 1988). It is difficult to say which is harder. Acquiring student skills, or in this case reacquiring them, means more than simply becoming able to sit still for long periods of time or take notes during lectures. It involves, among other things, retraining memory and developing the style of writing that the instructor or the system approves.

Above all, becoming a student requires a surrender of independent judgment, a deliberate deference to what is formally the judgment of the agency or system, though for the most part it actually is the view only of a few individuals who represent the system. In the advanced levels of the system, the relationship between student and structure at its best approaches the cooperative, but the residual power of the system's authority is always there. This surrender is hardly noticeable in the case of the young, who are dependent in so many other areas of their lives, but it becomes more visible and thought provoking in adult students, who are used to being and are expected to be self-determining.

Little thought has been given to the consequences of the emergence of a nation of students (Ohlinger, 1974). The fact that the population of adult students in all of the developed countries is composed primarily of those who have succeeded in the school system as children and young people suggests the power of the student role as it is maintained by that system: these people feel comfortable learning predominantly, perhaps only, in that role. A harsh assessment would be that this is a case, at least in part, of slaves having learned to love their chains.

It is impossible to escape the similarity between some aspects of the role of student and those of the role of employee. (Indeed, some socialist countries treat the two as nearly identical.) Observation of the life of graduate students, with their dependence on government fellowships, high grades, and "performance appraisals" by faculty, combined with the growth of research controlled by government funding, makes the similarities between students and employees especially plain. Perhaps the similarities have been there all along and we are only now being forced to recognize them.

The student role provides many benefits and satisfactions, but it also has its drawbacks. The limitations of this role most probably lie at the heart of the limitations of present systems of formal education, which seem to prevent these systems from having much effect on the primary dilemmas of our time. The educational system defines the types of learning outcomes that are expected for students, and these outcomes are not likely to be ones that produce paradigm shifts, perspective transformations, or conversions. Yet it is exactly these more profound types of learning objectives that seem to be most sought after today (Botkin, Elmandjra, and Maritza, 1979; Ferguson, 1980).

The student role offers some sharp contrasts with the role of learner. The learner is not totally free, of course, since he or she must surrender to the demands of what is to be learned and the existing skills and knowledge with which the learning task must be addressed. John Dewey (1961) argued, in defense of his concept of adjustment, that if one wishes to throw a stone, one must adjust the shape of one's hand to the shape of the stone. However, the learner needs to surrender only to these intrinsic demands, not to external demands regarding how, when, or where learning is to be accomplished. The student, however, is ruled primarily by external demands, as we have shown. Another vital distinction between learner and student is that the private learning program of the independent learner offers no public certification as long as it remains private, whereas the learning program of the student can result in public certification and all the advantages in terms of employment and so on that such certification brings.

Although both learning needs and educational needs arise constantly, they are likely to be more acute at some stages of individual and societal life than at others. The next chapter will examine these points of learning-related crisis, or "learning occasions," during which both governments and individual citizens perceive that most of the needs demanding to be met are in fact learning needs. These "learning occasions" present the most significant challenges to the successful management of learning.

4

The Learning Occasion: When and Why Learning Takes Place

Certain events arise in the life of every organization, including every society, in which learning becomes likely, indeed is almost required, to occur because learning needs are identified as the decisive needs of the group. We call such events "learning occasions." The chief learning occasions that we have identified are entry, passages, societywide changes, and exceptions (Thomas, Beatty, Ironside, and Herman, 1980). As with learning needs that appear at any other time, governments can respond to the needs generated by learning occasions by permitting, encouraging, directing, or forbidding the pursuit of particular learning objectives. (These responses will be discussed in detail in Chapters Five and Six.) Such learning management, as we have pointed out, has become much more conscious and complex in recent years.

Every society has to cope with the phenomenon of entry. The most common and obvious example of entry is the entry into society of children born to that society's existing members. The entry of "strangers," however, also has been a matter of societal concern since earliest times. Dealing with the latter means coping with the learning (on the part of both "strangers" and "residents") made necessary by the arrival of adults who come from outside the society.

The second major kind of learning occasion is the passage

from one life state or status to another—from a child to an adult, from a single individual to a partner in a marriage, and so on. New attitudes, skills, and knowledge associated with the new state must be learned as part of each passage. In early nomadic and agricultural societies, the types of societies in which humankind has lived throughout most of its history, life was short and life passages were few. Once the transition was made from childhood to formal adult status (usually at puberty), the only other passages that most people encountered were marriage, parenthood, and death. Perhaps simply because there were so few, the passages that did occur, especially the transition to adult life, usually were marked by elaborate public ceremonies. These societies felt that it was extremely important that both the individual and the community acknowledge the individual's assumption of, and right to exercise, newly learned skills and responsibilities.

Today most people in industrial societies live much longer than their forebears, and they occupy a more complex world. Some modern writers therefore hold that the number of passages in adult life has increased significantly (Sheehy, 1976). At the same time, the ceremonies marking the passages (if any) seem to have become more private and much less elaborate. Because celebration of most passages is no longer a community event, we have had to develop other means of discovering what specific status or role a particular person occupies at any given time. Examples include the use of formal titles based on education or occupation, such as Doctor or Senator, and the common party question, "What do you do?"

Societywide changes in earlier times were primarily of two kinds: those caused by nature (flood, drought, famine, plague) and those caused by human beings (invasion, war). The learning accompanying or following the first kind of change usually arose from trying to cope with the effects of the disaster, although attempts at prevention or at least prediction often also were made. In the latter type, learning was determined partly by whether the group was aggressor or victim. Historically, the management of the learning involved in societywide changes was entrusted to relatively small groups of people, usually religious specialists (shamans, priests), political specialists (chiefs, kings), or military specialists (generals, war chiefs). These people were required to learn more than other members of the society, and the society as a whole benefited (at least potentially) from their learning. Today's societywide changes, for example the women's movement or the introduction and spread of personal computers, tend to be more subtle and less obviously disastrous than the old ones, but the needs for learning that they generate are just as acute and far more pervasive. Everyone, not just an elite group, must learn how to deal with them.

Response to what we have called exceptions (people who require special responses because of physical or mental handicaps) has depended upon the nature of the group and its circumstances. Nomadic peoples usually were obliged to abandon their sick or physically handicapped members unless those people possessed some unusual capability. People afflicted with contagious diseases, such as lepers, were either driven away or exiled to special colonies so that they would not infect the bulk of the population. Presumably the principal learning challenge arising from exceptions was the need to detect these special cases and develop appropriate responses to them. Even in settled, industrialized societies, dealing with exceptions usually has been left to the voluntary activities of the Learning Domain.

Societies and smaller groups within them have responded to the demands of "learning occasions" in different ways. A study of present societal responses to these occasions and recent changes in those responses can reveal much about the way modern societies are striving to maintain themselves and the ways that governments have altered their modes of responses to their citizens' learning needs.

Entry

Anyone entering a new organization—which includes a new baby being born into a family or an immigrant entering a new country—must learn to cope with it, and the organization's members in turn must learn to cope with the entrant. The American novelist John Gardner once claimed that all fiction has only two basic roots: a young person leaving home to make his or her way in the world, and a stranger coming to town. Perhaps all learning could be said to stem from these same two situations.

The overt response of an organization to a newcomer may be as simple as a few introductions, a couple of handshakes, and a brief tour of the facilities. In contrast, Peters and Waterman in *In Search of Excellence* (1982) point out with considerable emphasis the attention that the successful corporations they studied paid to introducing new "members" (employees) to the subtleties of the organizations' individual "cultures." Nowhere in the world is the importance of organizational culture and the inculcation of all employees into that culture's "folkways" more clearly demonstrated than in Japan (Dore, 1973; Ouchi and Jaeger, 1978; Sutherland, 1986).

The response to entry in large organizations is sophisticated and complex and, as in the armed services, may last for a considerable period of time, though the purpose of the response is always to transform the newcomer into an asset to the group as quickly as possible. During the time of unofficial "apprenticeship" the newcomer is learning new procedures and skills and, above all, is being socialized to the ways of the organization. Perhaps no other aspect of life shows so clearly that learning involves duration.

Children. The most common form of entry in all societies is the arrival of newborn children. Here the "newcomers" not only must learn the ways of the society but also must be provided with protection until they have developed sufficiently to become independent. The chief vehicle for these services has been and remains the family, or some relatively small human group that performs the functions of a family. (Though the composition of families appears to be changing rapidly at present, all of the new configurations, such as households involving single parents or stepparents, appear to perform the same functions as traditional families [Boulding, 1981].) Most other approaches to the nurturing and socializing of small children have failed, and some even have caused the death of the children

(Rakoff, 1985). Even after a century of acceptance of state intervention in the lives of children beginning around five years of age, the necessity of the family's role in the earlier years of the child's life seems to remain unarguable.

Convictions regarding the critical importance of what is learned during this period of life are equally strong. Learning to be self-aware, to talk, to walk, to love, to learn—all occur during the child's first few years. Two factors appear to be overwhelmingly important for success in these crucial forms of learning: a close association between learning and loving (an association that will continue to be significant throughout the person's entire lifespan) and the essential privacy of the family life in which the learning takes place. Though the dimensions of what a society regards as private may change (and often have changed), the essence of privacy stems from its association with family life.

States have almost always provided some protection for some families (thus indirectly supporting the learning that goes on inside families), though there was little enough for the vast majority during the industrial revolutions. At that time the church rather than the state was perceived to be the major vehicle of family support and protection. During most of this century, nation-states have provided some tax relief for families and sometimes direct subsidies as well (the Canadian "baby bonus," for example), although the appropriate extent of government protection for families has been a subject of constant debate.

The entry of a child into the family, particularly the entry of a first child, requires considerable learning from the parents as well as from the child. There is an immense literature, almost all modern, devoted to helping men and women learn how to become fathers and mothers. There is an almost equally large literature (usually associated with the mental health of children, child abuse, and juvenile delinquency) devoted to examining and repairing the consequences of the failure of parents to learn these important roles successfully. Traditionally, instruction in the skills of parenthood has been provided by the characteristic forms of the Learning Domain—extended families, volunteer organizations, and churches. Recently there have been attempts to transfer this instruction to the Educational Domain through such vehicles as "family life instruction" classes, but these attempts have had only limited success.

When children's attendance in school became required by law in the early decades of this century, a major part of the management of learning associated with the entry of children shifted from the Learning to the Educational Domain. Children moved from an almost totally private existence to the public role of pupil at about five years of age. Since that time, the Educational Domain has extended itself to hold young people until later and later ages, and more recently the increased demands on the learning potential of the population, coupled with the feminist movement's demand for more child care, has tended to extend this domain's control to younger and younger children as well. Day-care services are not yet officially part of the educational system, but factors such as declining numbers of conventional pupils, underemployed teachers, and the ambitions of parents are likely to make them so in time.

There is no doubt of the needs of working parents and their children for adequate care, and it may well be appropriate for governments to provide at least some of this care, but there is considerable doubt that turning very young children into pupils is in their best interest. We believe that it would be wiser to leave children in roles appropriate to the Learning Domain and to make provision for them in the way familiar to that sector, that is, through financial assistance to private groups. Such groups are much more likely to provide a nurturing, familylike environment than is the public educational system.

No society can escape the learning needs created by the entry of children into its ranks. There are many ways to meet these needs, however, and the wholesale provision of public education is only one. In most world societies today the state has argued successfully that no family is capable of providing all of the instruction and socializing necessary for a new generation. It also has claimed that publicly supported education can benefit families by freeing children from the economic circumstances of their parents. On the contrary, however, evidence strongly suggests that state intervention in children's learning has served to weaken families even more than the onslaughts of industrialization. Once a child begins going to school, the authority of the school, the teacher, and increasingly the association with other children intervenes between that child and his or her family. The ideals, values, and expectations of school and family at least potentially come into conflict. The conflict was minimal as long as the cultures of the school and the family roughly coincided, but if these cultures do not coincide, as is most notably the case with immigrant families, the more powerful institution, the school, generally prevails. The family retreats, and the child must cope with the conflict.

Do we really intend for future citizens to believe that the only important, relevant learning occurs in school, as an outcome of the kind of learning procedures that the formal school represents? Everyday experience contradicts this assertion, yet the social force with which the idea is presented tends to illegitimize other forms and outcomes of learning and drive them "underground." This contradiction presently arises, for example, with regard to learning derived from broadcasting, which is not recognized by the schools but plays an extremely pervasive role in everyday life. The contradiction leads to a singularly destructive situation in which young people are denied the full use of immensely powerful sources of learning. The result corrupts the relationship between the educational system and its students because educators, preoccupied with what they are teaching, become blind to what is actually being learned.

The political control of the educational system, the principal relationship between the Social and Educational domains, has not served to correct these problems. At least until very recently, decisions made in the "citizenship" sector (the Social Domain) have served only to support and extend the exclusivity of the formal system of education (the Educational Domain) and underemphasize the value of learning associated with the Learning Domain. Despite these trends, there is impressive evidence that unless the Educational Domain becomes responsive to and reflective of the learning that is occurring in the Learning Domain, the former is in danger of withering away.

Today we need to reconsider the proper relationship of the Learning and Educational domains in preparing children for their entry into society. For a century we have believed that this task could best be done by the extension and maximization of the activities characteristic of the Educational Domain. It has become clear, however, that this view is no longer tenable. Each of the two domains provides a different experience with learning, and both kinds of experience are important to the development and socialization of the child. Both help children develop attitudes toward learning and ideas about how learning is accomplished and about what learning is appropriate and what is not under particular circumstances. The process of developing these attitudes and ideas is the most significant aspect of socialization.

Adults: Immigrants, Guest Workers, and Refugees. The second kind of "entry" that creates major learning needs in a society is the arrival of immigrants (both children and adults) or other strangers in a society. The literature associated with immigrants' entry and the related learning is among the most prevalent and poignant in any language. Examples that come to mind range from the Bible's *Book of Exodus* to Helen Waddell's *The Wandering Scholars* (1927) and C. Goodham-Smith's *The Great Hunger* (1962).

Individuals, families, and tribes have migrated from one place or society to another throughout history. Emigration often has been chosen as an alternative to meeting a learning need that arises from a societywide change, such as the need to acquire new agricultural skills because of a change in climate, the need to learn new martial skills in order to repel an invader, or, more recently, the need to develop new occupational skills because of industrialization or war. In fact, emigration simply exchanges one set of learning needs for another — those associated with overcoming a threat for those associated with entering and adapting to a new society.

Since the middle of this century, Western governments have been concerned principally with three types of new entrants: conventional immigrants, the "guest workers" of the European Common Market, and refugees. Canada, Australia, New Zealand, and (to a lesser degree during this period) the United

States have received substantial numbers of voluntary immigrants, most of which have intended to remain in their new countries permanently and become citizens. In contrast, members of the European Common Market have created the classification of "guest workers," people who are permitted, and in fact in the early stages of the program were encouraged, to enter countries other than their own for the purpose of finding employment. These workers usually do not bring their families to the new country, and there has been little expectation (with the recent exception of Sweden) or even opportunity for them to become citizens of that country.

The temporary form of immigration represented by guest workers would seem to involve only economic factors, but there is no clearer example of the fact that every living person is continuously both a learner and a source of learning for other persons. The mere presence of these people forced citizens in the host countries to learn about the immigrants' cultural and social characteristics (as well as, of course, vice versa). In fact, it is precisely the guest workers' role as sources of learning that has soured the arrangement in recent years, stimulating programs to induce them to return to their home countries.

The final adult group involved in entry is refugees. Torn from their old homes by war, famine, or some other disaster, refugees, like guest workers, usually have been expected to be relatively temporary residents of new countries; it has been assumed that they would return to their place of origin when the conditions causing their flight had abated. Yet the learning potential of all human beings means that they cannot live in suspension. If refugees remain in a host country long enough to begin a new generation there, most people in that new generation become full members, if not citizens, of the new country. Today potential host countries such as Australia and Canada tend to assume that refugees, such as those arriving recently from East Asia, will become permanent members of the societies to which they have fled (Greater Toronto Southeast Asian Refugee Task Force, 1981; Stock, Duke, Gundara, and Thomas, 1986). But this tendency, however well-meaning, to treat refugees in the same way as immigrants angers some refugees, who feel that having to accept the new country will weaken their determination to return home.

Both immigrants and refugees consist of mixtures of adults and children. In receiving these groups, host countries must prepare to respond to the learning needs of all ages. In addition, as in the case of children born into a society, entry is a two-way street: it creates learning needs in the citizens of the receiving country as well as in the new arrivals. At a minimum, these citizens must learn to bear the costs of the special provisions made for the newcomers; at the maximum, they must learn to accept, if not to welcome, the changes in the entire society associated with food, language, and public behavior that inevitably result from the inclusion of strangers. All of these demands provide considerable stimulation for the activities of the Learning Domain, in which the bulk of the adjustments work themselves out.

Different countries and governments intervene in this learning to different degrees and in different ways. With the exception of classes that teach language, however, governments have offered few formal educational opportunities to adult immigrants or refugees. What little was done educationally for these people depended, to a large extent, upon the provisions already made in the host society for the education of adults, which until the middle of this century usually were minimal (Stock, Duke, Gundara, and Thomas, 1986). Even most language instruction has been provided by the organizations and vehicles of the Learning Domain rather than by the formal educational system.

The most common government response to learning needs generated by the arrival of newcomers has been to include immigrant or refugee children in the system of compulsory education. The intent was that, whatever happened to the "newcomer" parents, their children would learn to be proper citizens of their adopted country. A considerable literature has developed around the problems associated with attempts to integrate such children into existing school systems, including the stresses that develop both within the schools and within the children's families.

The classic formulation by Thomas and Znaniecki (1974) of the "second-generation problem"—children of immigrants growing up with a sense of belonging to neither culture — has become universally accepted and has stimulated a variety of attempts to ameliorate its most destructive effects. This phenomenon is a direct result of formal schools in the receiving societies attempting to ignore immigrants' concurrent learning. Both the process and the outcomes of the learning that immigrant children experience in formal school contrast sharply with the learning experiences of their parents, which occur almost exclusively in the Learning Domain. These contrasts make intergenerational conflict inescapable. Newcomers' children enter the host country's educational system with little previous experience of the Learning Domain of that particular country, though they generally have experienced the intense learning involved in family life. Adult newcomers, by contrast, have had to depend almost entirely on the Learning Domain and lack any experience of the Educational Domain in the new country. They thus can do little to help their children cope with educational needs, and the result is frustration, misunderstanding, and anger for children and parents alike.

These problems are most intense when the newcomer families are poor. In terms of narrowly conceived academic success, the same pattern seems to prevail among immigrant children as among the native born. The children of well-off immigrant parents succeed, frequently exceeding the achievements of native-born children, while the children of poor immigrant parents do less well. It appears that the "culture" of school, despite variations in differing societies, is universal. Children of parents who have succeeded in society, particularly if those parents also have succeeded in school, are themselves likely to succeed in school (in strict academic terms, at least) even if the school is in a different society.

Newcomer Learning and Multiculturalism. Host countries have tended to assume that the environment of employment and civic life, coupled with access to language instruction, provides enough information to allow newcomers to be at least minimally integrated into the host society. For the most part, this assumption has proved correct, but it has had unexpected results. When the political environment of the host country includes freedom of speech, association, and learning, it allows the creation of social vehicles for living a cultural life that necessarily differs both from the life that would have been lived in the home country and from the prevailing life of the host country. The primary vehicle thus created is a so-called "ethnic group," an association of newcomers from a particular country that is controlled by its members and seeks to provide a range of services for them. The business of this informal association is conducted, for the most part, in the immigrants' original language.

If an ethnic group's numbers are sufficient, the services it supports can be extensive. For example, surveys showed that the first group of Italian immigrants arriving in Toronto after World War II believed that their highest priority should be to learn to speak English. Ten years later, however, Italians arriving in the same city no longer felt that learning to speak English was a prime necessity because they could find all the services they needed, including employment and living accommodation, in areas where almost everyone spoke Italian. Only during the economically stressful period of the late 1970s and early 1980s, when employment in the Italians' traditional occupation, construction, declined sharply, did many of these people find it necessary to learn to speak English in order to seek work outside the Italian enclaves.

Canada has a flourishing ethnic press and broadcasting system. The latter is of particular significance because it requires not only the economic support of ethnic group members but also the support of the government in allocating frequencies for broadcasting in languages other than the prevailing one(s). Similarly, freedom of movement has allowed sizable "ethnic" neighborhoods to develop, contributing further to the sustenance of language and folkways while at the same time preventing such neighborhoods from acquiring the worst characteristics of the traditional ghetto. Support for ethnic groups provided by their own members and, to some extent, by the greater society thus flourishes in Canada.

In addition to services provided for immigrants by volunteers from their own ethnic groups, other services often are

provided by volunteers from the host country who are sensitive
to the problems of resettlement. Both kinds of groups contribute to learning: the experience gained by newcomers in managing their own organizations is the most effective source for learning how to cope with the political, economic, and social "ways"
of the host country, and citizens' volunteer agencies help those
citizens learn to understand and to a degree accept the reality
of the newcomers as people with a distinct culture rather than
merely potential duplicates of the citizens themselves. A host
country's use of the voluntary services of both newcomers and
native born allows maximum flexibility for learning.

With two official languages and two visible cultures,
French and English, Canada has found it difficult, if not impossible, to present only one model of citizen for newcomers
to emulate. The result has been a great deal of tolerance, even
encouragement, for recent arrivals' maintenance of some aspect
of their original cultures. The United States has maintained a
much stronger policy of "assimilation," however.

It is very significant that within the last two years a bill
has been presented in the Senate that would make English the
official language of the United States. This proposal probably
was made because of the recent rapid proliferation of Spanish-
speaking (and perhaps Asian language-speaking) American
citizens and residents, a development both symbolically and
functionally acknowledged by the fact that both presidential can-
didates in 1988 spoke at some length in Spanish during their
acceptance addresses. The Senate bill and similar language protection legislation passed in the province of Quebec, like cor-
responding "English-only" bylaws passed in Ontario during the
same period, is an example of the societal response of forbidding learning, since it attempts to prevent people from using,
at least officially, any language except the designated one, with
all of the cultural and attitudinal characteristics that that language may carry. Since language, spoken and written, is a
primary vehicle for learning, equating language with citizenship is a profoundly significant move. Language lies at the heart
of any individual's sense of identity as person, citizen, and so
on, most of which has been learned.

In North America the sometimes reluctant acceptance of ethnic groups has been based on the assumption that such groups were temporary vehicles of resettlement that would last only one generation. Recently, however, the strength and tenacity of these groups and of their continued demand for services has led to the development of policies of "multiculturalism" (Stock, Duke, Gundara, and Thomas, 1986). Such policies depart dramatically from the early vision of the nation-state as representing one land mass, one nation, and one culture.

Recently Canadian policies of multiculturalism have been transferred to some extent from the Learning to the Educational Domain, first through language classes provided in the evenings for adults and subsequently through the introduction of "heritage language programs" for children in the formal system. Whether the nation can survive this remarkable experiment is an unanswered question. At the time of writing the conflicts it has produced are open and severe. Though the conflicts appear to be mainly between English and French cultures, the transfer of multiculturalism to the Educational from the Learning Domain is actually what is at stake. Without that transfer, the idea of multiculturalism is likely to remain a minor strand in the fabric of Canadian society.

An unusual example of the effects of multiculturalism can be found in Finland, where the native Finnish culture, dominated for centuries by the official Swedish culture, not only survived by reliance on the instruments of the Learning Domain but eventually replaced the Swedish elite (Jutikkala, 1979). Apparently a similar means of survival is being used by the Spanish-speaking people in the United States. Since few formal schools teach in Spanish or teach Spanish as a first language, we must conclude that the continuing increase in expressions of Spanish-speaking culture is entirely due to activities associated with the Learning Domain.

Immigrants, guest workers, and refugees clearly have used the Learning Domain in different ways. In the case of the two latter groups, expectations of impermanence have led to lesser development of the agencies that have served immigrants. It is difficult to assess with any accuracy the degree to which reliance on the Learning Domain has accomplished the intended goals of either immigrants, native-born citizens, or host country governments. One could argue, though hardly prove, that the recent civil disturbances in Britain, which involved large numbers of deprived immigrant minorities, are an indication of failure, showing that the host society had not provided sufficient support for the instruments of the Learning Domain.

It is impossible to know whether the multicultural policy now in favor in places like Canada will produce a new kind of cooperative nation-state or whether instead the various ethnic groups involved will develop a continuing sullen, "underground" conflict in which learning is depressed or even stifled completely. It is difficult, furthermore, to know what pattern of agency and program development in the Learning Domain is most likely to permit the required learning and achieve the intended goals. Nevertheless, the fact that most countries have relied principally on the Learning Domain to meet needs associated with adult entry is significant. Since the movement of peoples as refugees, guest workers, immigrants, and multinational employees is likely to continue to increase throughout the world, more serious attention must be given to the management of learning and to the relationships between the domains of learning and education in this connection.

Passages

For most of the world's history, each person who lived into adulthood normally underwent five major life passages: birth, adulthood, marriage, parenthood, and death. All of these passages were experienced within a relatively short time period, usually forty to fifty years. Until the middle of this century, even at the height of industrialism, the pattern did not change much, though some finer discriminations had been introduced. Childhood was divided into two periods, before entering school and after. Marriage became separated in time from parenthood as some couples delayed childbearing. Increasing longevity introduced a life stage called retirement, in which an older person might be healthy and active but no longer practiced the occupation that had provided income, status, and, to a large degree, identity. As the number and character of the recognized passages in life altered, so did societal views of "development."

As presently designated, life passages seem to be of two kinds. Some are primarily domestic or private, such as birthdays (even-decade birthdays, such as the thirtieth or fortieth, and the birthdays associated with legal assumption of adult rights often are held to be especially important), the departure of grown children from the home, and (sometimes) serious illness. Traditionally these private passages have been dealt with in the Learning Domain.

The second group of passages is more public in nature. It includes such events as entering school for the first time, acquiring a driver's license, marriage, childbirth, divorce (if it occurs), and death. In each case some formal public registration is required, and the event usually is accompanied by a semipublic celebration such as a wedding, a christening, or a funeral. A special subgroup in this category is made up of events associated with employment, such as hiring, promotion, changing of job or employer, firing (if it occurs), and, finally, retirement.

Traditionally the learning required by or associated with these semipublic passages, as with the private ones, has been provided and controlled by the characteristic agencies of the Learning Domain: the family, the church, and the employer (or organizations related to employment, such as unions). In the past two decades, however, individuals and groups increasingly have turned to the agencies of the Educational Domain for provision of this learning. In response, educational providing agencies have begun to offer formal instruction aimed at preparation for marriage, parenthood, retirement, and even death and dying. Similarly, employers increasingly have linked progress in employment to the achievement of some form of certification by the formal educational system. For understandable reasons this has been particularly true of the professions and would-be professions (in fact, an occupation's recognition by an educational agency, resulting in provision of training programs and licensing certificates, often has become the basis for its emergence as a profession).

Adolescence. In addition to dividing childhood into two parts, the pattern of universal schooling created an intermediate life stage between childhood and full adulthood that is commonly called adolescence or the teenage years. This stage did not exist in most earlier societies, in which a young person was considered ready for marriage and other adult responsibilities as soon as he or she reached puberty. The duration of "adolescence" has varied largely according to the demands of a society's economy, but (at least until recently, when growing numbers of adults began to reassume the student role), it more or less coincided in timing with the role of "student" in the Educational Domain. The beginning of adolescence may be marked by the occurrence of physical puberty, the first "teen" birthday, or entry into junior high or high school. Its conclusion is usually considered to be graduation from secondary school or college, or perhaps the birthday upon which certain adult rights and responsibilities (the right to vote, the right to drink alcohol, the responsibility to perform military duties or some other form of national service, and so on) are legally acquired. Young people in this life stage have more responsibilities than children, but they do not have the full rights and responsibilities of an adult citizen.

The Educational Domain officially has been held responsible for this group's learning, although a great deal of their learning in fact takes place outside this domain. Adolescents' experience in the Educational Domain was "preparatory" in the sense that it tried to anticipate what they would need to be, know, and do when the educational period was over. In addition, for most young people during the first half of this century, it was regarded as terminal; that is, they were expected to leave the Educational Domain permanently at the point of approaching or reaching adult status. All the rest of the learning they would need (and it was not expected to be much) was expected to be accommodated in the Learning Domain. In other words, assumption of adult status has been marked by, among other things, a transfer from the Educational Domain back to the Learning Domain. It often has been a difficult transition, partly because no one institution or group in the society has been willing to accept responsibility for it. As a result, millions of young people have been finding themselves less and less welcome in any sector: employers do not want them because they lack training and experience, school seems irrelevant to them, and families find them difficult to cope with.

The Passage to Adulthood. In many societies the passage from youth to adulthood has been marked by a short period of military service, primarily for young men but increasingly for young women as well. This is true in modern Israel, for example. Formal instruction during this period focuses on martial skills to be used in the defense of the country, but the learning that results from departure from the private context of home and participation in the intense collective environment of the armed services is of far greater consequences for the development of citizenship. Other societies such as Canada and the United States, which in recent years have not had compulsory military service, have resorted to similar but voluntary organizations to help young people achieve the learning associated with the passage to adulthood and identification with their nation. The Peace Corps in the United States and the now-defunct Company of Young Canadians are two examples of such voluntary organizations. Boy Scouts and Girl Guides (Girl Scouts), common to both countries, are others.

Citizens of industrial countries in recent years frequently have expressed concern over how the young learn to deal with the traditional passage from youth to marriage and parenthood. High rates of divorce and desertion, of childbirth out of wedlock, and, most recently, of demands for access to abortion frequently have been blamed on the failure of modern society to arrange for the learning needed for successful transition to these adult roles. The most persistent societal response to this criticism during the past half century, as we noted earlier in this chapter, has been to attempt to transfer responsibility for managing the required learning from families and perhaps church groups to the system of formal education, where instruction takes the form of courses called "Family Life" or similar titles.

The content and even the existence of such courses has

become the source of continuous dispute. For example, they have been accused of weakening or betraying the family because they place what has been regarded as quintessentially private and autonomous under the direction of a public authority (the teacher). Furthermore, even where these courses have been made a part of the official curriculum, there is little evidence of their success. They demonstrate the limited ability of formal education to handle matters that must be learned but cannot be taught. People usually have learned about family life by experiencing it, and this probably is still the best way. If "family life" courses do have a use, it is more likely to be for adults who have recently established their own families than for adolescents.

Adulthood and Employment-Related Passages. In the past twenty years, the work of Levinson (1978), Sheehy (1976), and others has suggested that there are more significant life passages, particularly in the adult years (approximately twenty to sixty years of age) than had previously been believed. Most such passages are of the private kind. Delineation of these passages has added to our understanding of the variety of learning occasions, since all such passages require that a person learn new responses and that those around him or her accept this learning need and the results of its fulfillment.

The view that adult learning will be minimal and will take place strictly in the Learning Domain (and some of the practices associated with this view) is now changing, thanks to the discovery of additional passages in life, increased support for lifelong learning, and, most practically, growing demands from employers and agencies of public safety for certification. Increasing numbers of adults therefore are turning to the Educational Domain for help in meeting the learning needs involved in negotiating life passages, especially those related to employment (Campbell, 1984; Devereaux, 1985). At the same time, a very extensive system of adult training and development, most of it provided by large employers and the armed services, has arisen in the Learning Domain ("Industry Report," 1987; Saint, 1974; Clark and Sloan, 1958, 1962, 1964, 1966; Eurich, 1985). Employee training programs will be discussed further in Chapter Five.

In employment two passages are of special interest: the entry into first employment and leaving employment for the last time, or retirement. In the past some division usually has been made between the provision of educational preparation for employment and employment itself. Once the preparation is completed, the individual is expected to find employment and the employer to find employees. Even in the socialist societies that guarantee employment, educational agencies for the young for the most part are operated by the state rather than by the employers, so even in these countries there is a distinct passage between education and employment.

In most societies in the past decade the numbers of people either entering or leaving the world of employment has increased dramatically, causing the state to intervene more often in these formerly relatively private matters. In the case of young people beginning employment, governments have utilized the Educational Domain by developing more programs at the former points of educational completion. Except for some cooperative programs, these efforts have not been very successful.

The growth in the use of the Educational Domain to meet learning needs related to employment usually has not resulted from deliberate public policy. Rather, it has arisen from the demands of large numbers of people who have taken advantage of the absence of quotas or age limits in the practices of the providing agencies. A decline in the numbers of conventional students and a commensurate surplus of educational resources have encouraged providing agencies to meet these demands.

Retirement and Old Age. Retirement, except when the state either enforces or forbids mandatory retirement at a particular age, usually has been a private matter between employer and employee. Particularly in industrial societies, the retired or elderly as a group until recently have tended to be classed among the impaired (our "exceptions" group) and as a result have been lumped together with the young as "dependents." In fact, the situation of many elderly people today is very different from that of either children or handicapped people, as advocates for the elderly frequently point out.

Many of today's older people (and more of tomorrow's) are both relatively healthy and reasonably well off economically. They have fulfilled their biological and career roles and have accumulated a great deal of experience in the process. They are still active as citizens, voters, and, to varying degrees, taxpayers. Most important in terms of their influence on society, they are still consumers. In a sense they are the first genuine leisure class. Yet neither they nor the other members of society who must respond to them have any satisfactory models to guide them in learning how to occupy these new roles. The number of such people is growing yearly, and their emergence as a separate group is likely to have profound effects on society. The passage into so-called retirement may eventually become as important as the passage of entry into employment. At present the learning related to it is handled fairly exclusively in the Learning Domain, but increasingly the elderly are demanding attention from the Educational Domain as well.

We can observe some dramatic shifts in the way that the various domains have been used to manage learning related to different life passages. At present there seems to be no way to be sure which approach is the most appropriate. The Learning Domain would seem to be the warmer, more immediately responsive of the domains, while the Educational Domain is the more systematic and rational. One problem is that the Educational Domain so far has responded chiefly to those who are willing to move through the educational system on its own terms and then demand more of the same type of directed learning. It has not been responsive to any great degree to those who wish to move in and out of the system or to achieve learning derived from a combination of the two domains.

Everyone goes through at least some of the passages of life, but people go through these passages at different times. As a result, only a relatively small number of people in any society are engaged in learning the same things at any one time. Occasionally, however, so many people are engaged in the same passage that it approaches the conditions of a societywide change. This has happened with all the passages undergone by the "baby boom" generation born in the late 1940s and 1950s. In the 1950s and early 1960s, when these young people entered school, societal preoccupation with formal education rivaled the preoccupation with war in the previous decade and with economic depression in the decade before that. Recently we have been hearing (endlessly, it sometimes seems) about this generation's maturity and midlife crises. When the "baby boomers" reach retirement age, the learning occasion related to passage into retirement and late life is likely to spawn needs that will take up many of society's learning (and perhaps educational) resources.

Societywide Changes

For our purposes, societywide changes can be placed into two categories. The first includes natural disasters such as floods, famines, fires, and epidemics of disease. The second encompasses changes (disastrous or otherwise) of human or social origin, such as religious movements, wars, revolutions, and movements for suffrage or freedom from slavery. Contemporary changes in this category, in addition to the century's various wars, include the feminist movement, the peace movement, the movement toward energy and resource conservation, and the increased emphasis on fitness and health.

By definition, societywide changes touch everyone in a society, though people may be involved in them to varying degrees. Such changes are the most dramatic part of history. Most historians, however, have emphasized the pain, suffering, and dislocation that these events cause rather than people's efforts, sometimes successful, to learn how to cope with them. During plague or fire, for example, the wealthy learn to abandon the city or village, while the poor learn to avoid the sick or the path of the flames as best they can.

Societywide changes are usually sudden and unexpected; the legendary "Four Horsemen of the Apocalypse," who symbolize the most spectacular of such changes, traditionally give little warning of their approach. Because of this quality, little teaching can be done about these events, so the involvement of the Educational Domain in the learning that they spark is minimal. Only when the immediate threat is over does some

aspect of the events enter formal teaching. Usually such teaching consists of recounting the history of the events in the hope
that future generations will learn how to prevent them or at least
to cope with them more effectively. Once the cause of contagious disease was understood, for example, students were taught
hygiene measures that could help to prevent the spread of such
disease.

Most responses to societywide changes, then, involve the
Learning Domain. These changes force everyone to learn to
change his or her behavior in some way. If the changes have
been disastrous, most learning will be directed toward trying
to restore the society to what it was before the disaster, for example by rebuilding damaged cities or reintegrating soldiers into
civilian life. Publicly the illusion of a return to the status quo
often works; privately, however, it must fail, because learning
is irreversible. Rubble may be removed and bodies buried, but
memory remains.

The same is true of learning connected with more subtle
societywide changes. During World War II, for example, the
withdrawal of millions of men from the economy caused large
numbers of women to learn skills and enter roles other than those
with which they had traditionally been associated. The attempt
to resume "normal life" after the war involved trying to persuade
these women to return not only to their previous roles but to
the belief that they had neither the ability nor the desire to learn
any others. This persuasion appeared to be successful during
the 1950s, but the seeds of new learning had been planted and
could not be eradicated. Those seeds burst into flower when a
new generation of women produced the feminist movement in
the 1970s.

Traditionally, peaceful human-caused societywide changes
in societies with freedom of speech and association begin with
the formation of voluntary organizations devoted to bringing
about such changes. Such organizations require at least some
of their numbers and supporters to learn the skills of organization, administration, and financing; that is, the skills needed
to focus the attention and energies of many people over a period
of time. The undertaking may be large and inclusive, like that

of the working-class Chartist protesters in Britain in the nineteenth century or the more recent movement in the United States
for black civil rights, involving petitions, bonfires, marches, and
demonstrations. Alternatively, it may focus on attracting relatively small numbers of influential people, like the turn-of-the-
century British socialist Fabian Society (George Bernard Shaw
was a famous member), which relied on the editorial, the white
paper (government report), and the select committee (Trevelyan,
1945). In recent years, perhaps because of the growth of television, large organizations and dramatic methods seem to pre-
dominate.

Whether large or small, groups seeking societywide change
tend to state their missions in terms of idealized objectives or
goals. They might be better advised to state them in terms of
what must be learned, how it can be learned, and by whom it
should be learned. Such groups frequently attribute opposition
to their cause to indifference or obstinacy, whereas the real problem may be a lack of sufficient information explaining why the
change they seek is necessary, a lack of opportunity to acquire
the skills needed to accomplish the change, or both. It seems
probable that many campaigns for societywide change fail at
least partly because their leaders do not recognize the pivotal
role that learning plays in achieving their goals.

Although most societywide changes emerge independently
of the state, the sponsors of such changes often attempt to win
the support of the state so that the changes they advocate may
be moved to the Social Domain and thereby become embedded in the structure of the society as not only desirable but required ways of behaving. The women's movement in the United
States, for example, tried (albeit unsuccessfully) to have equal
rights for women guaranteed legally by the proposed Equal
Rights Amendment to the Constitution. Learning resulting from
societywide changes eventually is incorporated into the Educational Domain as well, where it becomes part of the required
socialization of future generations.

Evidence that the Educational Domain is trying to cope
with societywide change can be seen in the recent proliferation
of short courses, provision for continuing education among

professionals, symposia, conferences, and the like, all aimed at helping adults learn how to deal with such changes. Presumably such programs are presented both because of the providing institutions' sense of responsibility and because of their need to attract new clienteles. Educational providing agencies do represent substantial repositories of knowledge, skill, and resources. They are not well equipped to handle the challenge of societywide change, however, because the commitment of most of these agencies (except for universities) strictly to teaching, and therefore to including material in their programs only after it has been learned and practiced elsewhere, runs directly counter to the kind of experimental, learning-based responses that societywide changes require. The reward systems, financial practices, and administrative structure of formal educational institutions all lean unequivocally toward the predictable, the measurable, and the dependable. To some extent we treasure these institutions for precisely these characteristics. Nonetheless, such characteristics make the educational system likely to remain marginal in helping people deal with societywide changes, especially in the early stages of these changes.

Governments, too, sometimes seek to bring about societywide change. During the first half of this century many states concentrated such efforts on the Educational Domain and thus on children — the next generation. The two world wars, however, provoked massive government intervention in the Learning Domain. These wars constituted societywide changes because they were both total and popular. They were total in that all of the participants' resources had to be directed to the objective of winning, and millions of nonprofessional combatants had to be enlisted. They were popular in that the bulk of the participant countries' populations voluntarily supported the wars' prosecution. (By contrast, the war in Vietnam was neither total nor popular for the United States, but it was both for the then North Vietnam.)

The governments involved in the world wars found that the enormous amount of learning needed to carry out these wars could best be generated by relying on the mechanisms and attitudes of the Learning Domain. However, the governments also learned that considerable skill was required to win and coordinate the voluntary support of individuals and organizations. For example, the government of Canada created the Wartime Information Board as a vehicle for winning the support of volunteer organizations. The board provided accurate information about the war effort and about the effect of the contributions of particular agencies to that effort (Young, 1978). Even totalitarian governments found that persuasion worked much better than compulsion in producing the learning that they desired. Many of the strategies for the encouragement of learning that governments developed first in wartime are now being used to cope with more peaceful societywide changes.

Governments are likely to need to use more and more of the mechanisms of the Learning Domain to handle societywide changes in the future, but they will have to develop the techniques to do so effectively. These include the skills of consulting, provision of sufficient information to allow objectives and the means for achieving them to be understood fully, allowance of adequate freedom in determining strategies for achieving objectives, and provision of information about the results of specific actions. On the surface these do not appear to be the techniques that win elections, and, until very recently, they have not been counted among the skills needed by public administrators. When they are considered fully, however, they can be seen to be the skills of a civilized and responsible life and the skills necessary for the effective management of learning. If governments will utilize these skills, as increasing numbers do, both government employees and the citizens who deal with such employees will acquire the skills as well. Both parties, and the country as a whole, will benefit from the improved opportunities for learning that such skills provide.

Exceptions

All societies, and many organizations within those societies, contain people whose behavior (often through no choice of their own) differs from the societal norm and for whom special provision therefore must be made. To an increasing degree, societies are judged by their willingness to provide for the special learning that must take place in order to accommodate these people.

These "exceptional" individuals can be divided into two groups in terms of the type of response they demand from society. The first group consists of people who have physical disabilities, including those caused by illness or age. Some early societies, especially nomadic ones faced with limited resources, found it necessary to abandon such people. As societies gained more control over their environments, however, they became more willing and able to provide for people who could not care for themselves. Ironically, most of these provisions until recently were made for children, which helped to guarantee that such children would live to grow up and face a world in which no further provision for them was made. Vanier's (1979) work in France with the adult retarded, who had been confined to lunatic asylums before his intervention, is an example of a new concern for exceptional adults. His creation of self-contained communities of retarded individuals showed that such people could learn to look after themselves and assume much greater control of their own affairs than had been thought. It demonstrated what could be learned and by whom in order to offer disabled people more rewarding lives.

The second group of "exceptional" people is composed of individuals with mental and emotional disabilities. Feelings about these people have been ambivalent because of disagreements about how much of their aberrant behavior, particularly behavior that is judged to be criminal, is under their control. For these reasons, the will to learn special responses or make special provisions for people in this group has developed more slowly and haltingly than the will to help people with physical disabilities.

In considering how to deal with exceptional people we again encounter the fact that learning is a two-way street. The disabled must learn (and must be helped to learn) how to cope with their disability. Such learning allows these people to take a relatively full part in society rather than being isolated or forgotten. More normal members of society, in turn, must learn to accept disabled people as part of everyday life by, for example, paying for the construction of ramp entrances or special washrooms in buildings or by learning how to converse with a person who is paralyzed or has cerebral palsy.

Virtually all of the learning associated with exceptional people occurs in the Learning Domain. The vehicles for this learning are frequently large voluntary organizations devoted to helping people with particular illnesses or disabilities. More recently, organizations made up exclusively of the disabled themselves have introduced new elements of service and advocacy in this area. Governments, too, have begun to replace old policies of segregating the disabled in specialized residential facilities with new programs intended to "mainstream" such people into the general society. These programs deliberately draw on the special resources and characteristics of the Learning Domain. Some of their lack of success so far may arise from the fact that the very nature of government makes it difficult for governments to work cooperatively with Learning Domain agencies.

The learning occasions with which all societies and groups must cope, as we have argued, can be said to be intersections of two-way streets. The rituals with which the classic learning occasions, especially those of life passages, have been associated are designed to remind us that not only the principals involved, who are concluding one period in their lives and commencing another, but also those of us who are associated with them must learn to adjust to their new circumstances. The bar mitzvah, the wedding, and the christening signal to individuals and the small groups that surround them what the demonstration, the special committee report, or the change of government administration signal to the society at large: new learning must be undertaken.

Except for the learning involved in the entry of children, almost all of the learning inspired by the crucial societal "learning occasions" has taken place in the Learning Domain. Today, as we have shown, learning occasions are increasing in number and variety. Each acts to multiply the learning needs of a society's members. If we are to retain order while at the same time mobilizing our societies by means of learning to a degree never before imagined, we must understand how we have managed the learning demanded by these occasions in the past and try to determine how best to manage it in the future. The next chapters will look more systematically at the ways societies and governments have responded to learning needs and managed their citizens' learning.

 5

Societal Responses
to Diverse Needs
for Learning

People form groups in order to try to meet their needs more effectively. Because (so far as is known) there has never been a time in world history when it was possible to meet fully all the needs of every living person, these groups have always existed in an atmosphere of scarcity. Each group, therefore, has tried to order the pursuit of need satisfaction so that most of the basic needs of most of the group's members could be met most of the time.

Chief among the groups that must regulate their members' attempts to satisfy needs are governments. Because the nation-state is the most common form of government in our contemporary world, our analysis will focus on this form, but we believe that our basic ideas could apply to any group at any period of history.

Governments must mediate between the individual and the collective pursuit of need satisfaction that takes place in the Social Domain. For example, city governments often must mediate between individuals' desire to use and change their residences in various ways and neighborhood groups' desire to maintain certain standards in order to protect their collective "quality of life" and property values. Governments must also mediate between competing activities of different groups and, to some extent, different individuals. Much of a government's activity is devoted to deciding which of whose needs will be met and how.

As an example of competing needs, suppose that a factory decides to try to save money (which can then be used to meet its members' needs and the needs of the business as a whole) by refusing to install equipment to remove dangerous chemicals from its waste water before the water is released into a nearby river. Residents of a town on the river form a group to protest the resulting pollution. Citing their need for clean water, they demand that the factory install water purification equipment. The factory management, in turn, says that the factory's water is only one source of pollution in the river and that the town should pay for a new sewage treatment plant to purify all the water discharged into the river. It insists, furthermore, that if it has to spend a substantial amount of money on new equipment, it will be forced to lay off a substantial number of workers, thus depriving the community of jobs and revenue.

Some government (local, state/provincial, or federal) is likely to have to mediate between these competing demands. Part of the government's decision may involve identifying certain of the needs involved as learning needs and considering ways to pursue their satisfaction. For example, workers who know how to operate the appropriate equipment will be needed for either the sewage plant or the new antipollution devices in the factory. In addition, building a sewage plant will require engineers, construction workers, and others who have the skills necessary for such a project. More of some of these types of workers may be available locally than others. This availability will affect the cost of the competing projects, since training workers in the skills needed or bringing skilled workers in from a distance probably will cost more than hiring local workers who are already trained. The government may therefore choose the project for which more local workers with appropriate skills are available. If too few skilled workers can be obtained for either project, the government may need to decide whether training local workers or hiring distant ones is a better choice.

Responding directly or indirectly to learning needs and trying to guide attempts to meet those needs make up a large part of any government's daily business. When governments make decisions about learning needs, they are mediating between the demands of competing individuals and groups in the Learning Domain much as they do in the Social Domain.

A government, like an individual, may identify certain needs as learning needs, or such needs may be identified first by a citizen or group of citizens who bring them to the government's attention. For example, a campaign for health improvement might need people to learn to give up eating fatty foods or smoking cigarettes. A campaign for environmental protection might stress the need for people to learn recycling and other new habits of waste disposal. Many political decisions require government officials to choose between competing learning needs, providing support for some but not for others. Governments try to make such decisions in a way that will ensure that individuals' learning will contribute to the general stability, morality, and well-being of the society as they conceive those things (Richmond, 1946).

Learning needs to which governments must respond may involve all or nearly all citizens, as with environmental protection and energy conservation, or they may demand learning only from a particular segment of the population. When a nation goes to war, for example, all of its fit young male citizens (and sometimes its fit young female citizens as well) are persuaded, with varying degrees of implied coercion, to learn an enormous range of military skills for which no need had been perceived before. The learning done by this group is expected to benefit the entire society. Government focus on the learning needs of children and youth in a sense involves both part and all of the population, since young people are not only part of the population at any given time.

Government Management of Learning

When a government (or, more precisely, the individuals who represent it) makes decisions about how to deal with its citizens' learning potential and their demands for the satisfaction of various learning needs, it is managing their learning. All governments have had to manage learning to some extent, but this was a much less major concern for earlier governments than it is for those of today. When those early governments did make decisions about learning management, such decisions were likely to affect only a relatively small number of people. That situation has changed greatly during this century.

Management of child learning, for example, until the twentieth century was commonly left to the family and, often, to religious agencies. In Europe and elsewhere, these agencies usually received protection and special privilege from governments partly because they were seen as the principal vehicle for meeting what was perceived to be the most important of all learning needs, the need to learn about God. The church, in fact, was for many centuries one of the principal vehicles for meeting learning needs of all types.

By the end of the last century, however, governments began to involve themselves increasingly in deciding how to provide for the learning needs of children until, by the middle of this century, state control of that function became total nearly everywhere in the world. During this period governments and private citizens alike widely believed that provision for the learning needs of children and youth, exclusively by means of formal education, would suffice to meet all the principal learning needs of the society. Experience showed, however, that this belief was far from correct. Partly because of the failure of formal education to meet many learning needs, states have increased substantially their identification of learning needs among all segments of their populations, and concern with such needs is now considered to be a regular function of government in most countries.

With that concern has come a multitude of new and sometimes vexing political problems. Futurist writers sometimes group these problems under the rather vague rubric of "turbulence." They may not have fully appreciated that turbulence is an inevitable characteristic of any society in which many people of all ages are learning, as is increasingly true in all societies today.

Every modern government knows that most of its major policies inevitably require involving some segment of a country's population in learning. This situation introduces new difficulties for the government. To begin with, it creates a relationship between the state and the citizen in which compulsion is of no avail, since learning cannot be coerced. Only individuals can learn, and learning requires an act of individual will. Governments can persuade, entice, or threaten, but they cannot command achievement of specific learning outcomes. A state must win — must earn — its members' will to direct their learning potential toward certain objectives. A state that fails consistently in that goal will surely disappear.

Second, a government must learn to deal with the fact that learning takes time. Learners frequently develop considerable loyalty to the source of their learning, but this may occur too late to benefit the particular government administration that made the learning possible. Finally, no one can predict the precise outcome of learning, no matter how carefully the need and the desired results have been defined. For example, few of the supporters of universal, compulsory state education for youth would have predicted the creation of "teenagers" and their attendant culture, yet that culture is clearly the result of segregating so many individuals of a similar age for purposes of education.

The threat of the problems that can arise from attempts to manage learning may explain why governments during the past century have tried so hard to avoid responding to learning needs. One form of avoidance is substitution, or seeking alternative sources of required skills or knowledge. In industry the two forms of substitution are called "make or buy": that is, a company that lacks workers with certain needed skills can either train existing employees in the desired skills ("make") or search the labor market for new workers who possess these skills ("buy"). The water pollution example at the beginning of this chapter included a choice of this kind. The "make or buy" choice can apply to objects (training materials, for example) as well as human beings.

Capitalists of the last century and the early part of this one traditionally chose the "buy" approach. This was quite feasible when most technologies required skills of only modest complexity. As technologies grew more complicated and specialized, however, the need for training and education specific to a particular industry or even a particular company increased. Some technologies today (some aspects of computers and of biotechnology, for example) are so new and complex that workers with sufficient skill or knowledge to operate in them simply do not exist (Clark and Sloan, 1958, 1962, 1964, 1966; Eurich, 1985). A company working in such an area has no choice but to provide the training and education required to "make" employees with the necessary skills.

The "immigrant" societies of this century (Canada, the United States, and Australia, for example), facing the twin pressures of empty territory and a lack of workers with desirable skills, found "buy" as attractive an alternative as the early capitalists did. The example of Canada is spectacular. That country emerged from World War II with a sense of confidence in its unlimited potential combined with a realization of serious current economic problems. These problems were, first, a need to increase the country's capacity to process and manufacture goods from the abundant raw materials it possessed (rather than simply exporting those materials unprocessed to the larger industrial countries) and, second, a need to increase its population.

A report of a Royal Commission in the late 1950s (Gordon, 1958) argued that while Canada's natural resources and investment capital seemed unlimited, the skilled work force required to allow the creation of a processing sector was not. There simply were not enough existing Canadian workers who had the required skills. At the same time, European countries were still suffering economically from the aftereffects of the war, but they had continued to train and educate their young people throughout the conflict. They thus had more trained workers than they had jobs.

Logically, then, Canada imported the skilled workers it needed from Europe — workers whose skills had been developed at the expense of other national economies. It is interesting to speculate about what sort of society Canada would be today if Britain, France, and Germany, her principal sources of skilled immigrants in the 1950s, had insisted, as the Soviet Union does, that emigrants must repay the cost of their education before they depart. At the very least, it would have caused the Canadian government and Canadian employers to learn much sooner to include training costs in their calculations. In point of fact they did not do so.

They also did not provide any appreciable training for their native-born workers, who remained virtually unskilled. The Canadian population and economy both grew for twenty-five years, but they did so at the expense of these unskilled native-born workers and at the expense of recurring problems of adjustment in employment. During that period, for example, demand for skilled workers in a region frequently coincided with large-scale unemployment in that same region, a problem that could have been solved if Canadian employers, like those in countries such as West Germany, England, and Japan, had been willing to spend money on training the unskilled native-born unemployed rather than importing, or "buying," workers from elsewhere who already possessed the needed skills. Canada did not entirely escape the problems associated with "making," however, since the arrival of these hundreds of thousands of immigrants made it necessary to provide them with widespread opportunities for learning, especially instruction in French or English. One set of learning needs thus was merely substituted for another.

In cases where substitution would not work as a way of avoiding a response to learning needs, governments usually have tried to shift learners from the Learning Domain to the Educational Domain (that is, to translate learning needs into educational needs) as quickly as possible. The careful direction of learning that constitutes education gives a government the illusion of control and the promise of a minimum of surprises. Only in the past decade has it become apparent, in light of such reports as UNESCO's *Learning to Be* (Faure, 1973), what the real consequences of the shift from learning to education are and how illusory is the control it promises. The structure of the formal educational system, the contradictions within it, and the consequence of using it as a response to learning needs will be discussed in the next chapter.

States can respond to learning needs and their citizens' learning potential by permitting, encouraging, directing, or forbidding the pursuit of particular learning objectives. In this chapter we will discuss permitting, forbidding, and encouraging as forms of learning management. These are the responses most likely to be applied to learning in the Learning Domain, whereas the directing of learning is the province of the Educational Domain.

It is appropriate to consider government responses to activity in the Learning Domain first because this area is both the more elusive and the more important of the two. The low visibility of activities in the Learning Domain makes them as hard for a government and its agents to spot as they sometimes are for citizens. Recent events in Burma, China, and other countries have reminded us that the inescapably high visibility of agencies in the Educational Domain leave them extremely vulnerable to government attack or censorship. The characteristic activities and agencies of the Learning Domain may be less vulnerable. For example, university education in Poland survived on a private, essentially "underground" basis during World War II, when the official universities were closed. "Popular educators" in Latin America function today in a similar way. In cases like these, educational efforts are widely diffused and embedded in other activities such as agriculture, community development, and urban renewal, making it even more difficult than usual for governments to detect what citizens' actual learning objectives are.

It seems apparent that the most dramatic outcomes of learning—conversion, perspective transformation, or paradigm shift (James, 1961; Mezirow, 1979)—are likely to occur only in the Learning Domain. This may be because of the proximity of activities in this domain to action and the high risks of failure, because of the warmth and loyalty associated with genuine membership, or, most likely, because so much learning in this domain does not take place as the result of explicit teaching. Learning that results from teaching has predetermined, and usually socially acceptable, goals, whereas learning that results from collective action is unpredictable and continually challenges the status quo. It is in the Learning Domain, therefore, that we must look for the sources of social change. Schools do not alter societies; on the contrary, they usually sustain and even intensify societal values. As we become more and more dependent upon people learning outside of educational institutions, schools are likely to decline even further in importance as originators of change. Management of learning in the Learning Domain therefore presents the principal challenge for any contemporary society.

Permitting and Forbidding Learning: Learning and the Law

Procedures for making governmental decisions about competing activities in the Social Domain are to be found in the laws of a country: constitutions, bills of rights, summaries of accepted practice (common law), and the like. Laws are creations of both the state and the government. The state is the contemporary order in which all citizens of a country live, whereas the government (or administration) is those groups or individuals who are in charge of the state at any one time. The state determines what learning will be permitted by, for example (in the democratic states), guaranteeing freedom of speech, association, and religion, all of which help to assure the underlying freedom of an individual to learn. Particular governments go beyond these basic freedoms by passing specific laws and taking other actions that support some learning objectives and discourage others. A state's overall body of law, which is the procedural architecture of that society, must reflect an image of individual human beings as both learners and stimuli to learning (actual or potential) at all times. Law is therefore a prime example of an area that is not normally thought of in terms of learning but upon which a learning perspective can provide important new insights.

The most fundamental job of a state in permitting learning through law is the maintenance of order and stability. Little of any developmental value can be learned in periods of extreme instability or violence. When groups or nations go to war with one another, they "freeze" in their relationships. Violence is the denial of learning; killing is its extinction.

In their search for what might be called "developmental order," the most advanced democratic states try to maintain structures that maximize the use of citizens' learning potential in the conduct of public affairs. For example, the use of courts with more than one judge, as in the highest courts in most countries, or of juries or multimember investigative tribunals reflects a belief in the value of the learning potential of more than one person for the pursuit of truth and justice. Perhaps the American structure of "checks and balances" is the world's most formidable example of the commitment to the value of multiple sources of learning as the basis for government.

Societies that place nearly absolute power in the hands of a few individuals, such as military dictatorships, present a sharp contrast to the preceding. In these societies the danger of a limited number of decision makers is frequently compounded by a rigid hierarchy and minimal opportunities for learning. The point is not that such governmental arrangements are morally wrong, although they may be, but that they are rarely successful in producing either stability or growth in a society. They fail because they cannot get a large enough number of citizens to want to pursue a wide enough range of learning objectives.

Two aspects of the legal foundations of modern societies are of interest here. One is the particular character of the legal system on which a society depends. For example, the system of common law, so characteristic of Britain and most of its former colonies, has at its core the belief in an individual's freedom to engage in any activity that is not expressly forbidden. This leaves citizens free, for the most part, to determine their own learning objectives and the best ways of meeting them.

In contrast to countries founded on common law are countries such as France and all socialist societies, which base their legal systems on what is called "normative law." Laws in these countries offer definitions of ideal behavior or human relationships. Normative law determines the goals of the society it governs, and it also determines what ought to be learned by each of the society's citizens. (To be sure, in practice such laws may tolerate a certain amount of deviation from the ideal, though in some countries, such as present-day Iran, tolerance seems to verge on the nonexistent.)

It is true that no society operates exclusively on the basis of one or the other of these types of legal code. Most common-law societies have regulatory tribunals that attempt to maintain some type of legislated "ideal" behavior, and most normative societies leave some areas of life undefined and behavior in these areas unmandated. The relationship between learning and the law is complex. It is also marked by potential conflict in that the function of the law is to define and fix behavior, whereas learning demands freedom to change and engage in novel behavior.

The second interesting aspect of the law is to be found in charters or bills of human rights. The importance for learning of the freedoms commonly embodied in such charters, such as freedom of speech, association, and movement, is obvious. We have already emphasized the importance of group membership and of other people to learning and thereby pointed out that freedom of association may be the most significant freedom of all from a learning point of view.

Freedom from discrimination, however, is almost equally valuable. While the focus of laws related to such freedom may vary (language is a major topic in Canada, for example, while in the United States little attention has been paid to this issue so far), almost all such compilations contain a common core of categories upon which discrimination is not permitted to be based. They include color, race, gender, place of origin, and age. What these categories (with the possible exception of gender, which is subject to sex-change operations and concomitant learning of the role of a different gender) have in common is that all are conditions that cannot be changed by learning, that is, by an act of individual will. Most modern democratic states agree that it is unfair to discriminate against people on the basis of conditions that they did not choose and cannot change.

Any of the four forms of learning management can be encoded in a country's laws. Laws demanding compulsory school attendance relate to the direction of learning, for example, and laws mandating expenditure of tax money on libraries or on training programs for unemployed youth relate to the encouragement or support of learning. Laws, however, are most often concerned with the permitting or forbidding of learning.

Citizens' freedom to pursue the satisfaction of learning needs is built into the procedural fabric of democratic societies. The government's task in such societies is merely to ensure that the rules that have been established are obeyed. It also must provide and maintain basic services, such as transportation and communication, that contribute to increased exchange among citizens and thus to opportunities for learning. Protection and promotion of freedom of association, as we have suggested, should be the most important aspect of a government's support of the permission to learn that is provided by law.

Most citizens of Western democracies take protection of freedom of association for granted, but a somewhat uneasy relationship between governments and smaller groups within the society always remains to threaten it. From time to time a government identifies some group as embodying learning objectives that the government perceives to be a threat to the dominant beliefs of the society or even the structure of the state itself. This happened to the Communist Party (and any groups or individuals suspected of being associated with it in any way, however indirect) in the United States during the infamous "McCarthy era" of the 1950s, for example. When a government identifies a group's learning objectives as a threat, the government, usually (though not always) following established procedural rules, attempts to forbid, even to eliminate, the pursuit of those particular learning objectives. It often creates new laws to aid it in this task.

Forbidding learning is never easy. Indeed, unless an alternative learning goal that is acceptable to the population is found, such suppression almost invariably fails. Rome's attempt to suppress Christianity failed; the Spanish Inquisition's attempt to suppress all disagreement within the Catholic Church (let alone expression of any religious opinion that fell outside that body of belief) failed; Hitler's attempt to suppress the Jews and all groups who opposed him failed. More contemporary failures include the attempts to restrict the learning associated with the nonmedical use of drugs (Leary, 1968) and with materials deemed to be pornographic. These latter attempts have succeeded only in producing continual conflict between authorities and certain citizens who seem determined to pursue such learning (not to mention those who seek to meet these people's learning needs at immense profit). Learning exercises a powerful attraction. A government may end the learning of particular individuals by killing them, but in the long run it is unlikely to suppress the pursuit of any particular learning objective completely.

Encouraging Learning

Most individuals and groups have little contact with the government in the course of their pursuit of particular learning objectives. In most contemporary states, however, if people wish to pursue public objectives, for example by engaging in commercial activities or lobbying for some social goal, they must register themselves publicly and acknowledge their principal officers and location. Groups pursuing such objectives are involved with learning in two major ways: first, their members or participants must learn the skills needed to maintain the groups and help them pursue their goals, and second, the groups may advocate the pursuit of certain learning goals that they believe are significant for the entire society. It has not been sufficiently recognized that the strength and longevity of such voluntary groups is related directly to the degree to which they provide learning opportunities for their members.

All governments possess a wide range of direct and indirect mechanisms for encouraging or supporting the learning activities of groups whose objectives the governments find to be in accord with their own interests and those of their society. For example, Richmond (1946) points out that the various Navigation Acts and regulations for the protection of fisheries introduced in England during the reigns of Henry VII, Henry VIII, and Elizabeth I actually were designed to ensure a steady supply of trained seamen for the English navy. The fishing industry was often called "the nursery of the navy." Governments have helped the members of both for-profit and nonprofit groups in their pursuit of certain learning objectives.

Aiding the For-Profit Sector. Since the turn of the century the principal form of government support for profit-making groups has been the supplying of trained workers who have acquired at least some of their skills as children at public expense. Underlying the seemingly endless debate in societies with extensive public education systems about whether or not their graduates are properly trained for employment and about who benefits most from such training, the employer or the potential employee, is the recognition by all parties of the fact that some form of preparation for employment is the principal objective of the educational system.

The educational system may have worked well for this purpose during the first half of the present century, but it is increasingly clear that it is not working well now and will not do so in the future. The idea that skills acquired at school or by means of apprenticeship in youth will suffice for a lifetime of employment has been untenable for at least twenty-five years, though specific practices adjusting to that fact have been slow to develop. For one thing, technologies and the skills needed to deal with them are constantly and rapidly changing today. For another, the fact that certain technologies and their attendant skills are limited to particular industries or even particular companies (Thomas, Beatty, Ironside, and Herman, 1980) has meant that few, if any, school systems can hope to find the resources to equip themselves to teach all of these technologies and skills. Both of these factors have caused considerable confusion to arise about what formal educational systems should be doing to prepare workers for employment and what resources they should provide for these workers' further training.

Large businesses have inaugurated extensive training programs for their employees, beginning as early as the 1920s (Clark and Sloan, 1958, 1962, 1964, 1966; Eurich, 1985). A United States survey of in-house training and education in the largest corporations estimated that total expenditures for such training would reach at least $4.2 billion in 1984. If smaller organizations were added and the cost of salaries and wages paid to employee-trainees were figured in, the estimate probably would exceed $20 billion (United States Training Census and Trends Report, 1982, 1983, 1984). Furthermore, the figure quoted excludes the armed services, as do comparable figures from other countries. The omission is significant because in times of relative peace, learning (training soldiers for a possible future war, as opposed to fighting a present one) is the chief preoccupation of the military everywhere.

Governments have supported pursuit of the learning objectives of future employees and their employers in a variety of ways. They commonly make the cost of training programs tax deductible, for example. Britain, France, and some other European countries have introduced schemes whereby employers and the government in effect divide the cost of retraining employees. In France, for instance, a tax is levied on the payroll of employers with more than a very small number of employees. The employer must either spend this money on the training of his or her employees within the calendar year or pay it to the state. Britain has used a variety of "levy-grant" systems, in which employers in a designated group are required to pay proportional sums toward the collective training costs of all employees in the group, part of which are also covered by the government. Several new programs in Canada involve direct government subsidization of employee training programs offered by employers. All such programs reflect the conviction that the cost of employee training should be shared between government and employers. This method of paying learning costs for adults presents an interesting contrast to the paying of the costs of children's learning through general tax revenues.

In addition, most European countries have established systems of "paid educational leave" for individual employees, either by statute or by collective bargaining. Such systems differ in detail, but basically they entitle every worker to a specific number of "educational days" throughout the year that may be taken without loss of pay, position, or benefits. In Canada, large employers make extensive use of such leave, but the timing and purpose of the leave are determined entirely by the employers. One major union, the Canadian Auto Workers, has bargained successfully for the individual use of such leave by its members, but no widespread agreement about introducing leave as an individual right has been reached, despite two extensive investigations (Adams, Draper, and Ducharme, 1979; Skill Development Leave Task Force, 1983; National Advisory Panel on Skill Development Leave, 1984).

It should be noted that the introduction of paid educational leave, whether by statutory provision or as a result of collective bargaining, has taken place against a background of a decline in the demand for reduced working hours. The utilization of educational leave means more time spent away from the workplace, just as do shorter working hours, but it also means that that time is devoted to the pursuit of learning objectives determined, in part, by other persons, such as supervisors or the leaders of labor organizations, whereas the time released by shorter work hours presumably could be spent in any kind of learning or other activity that the worker wished. The surrender of individual learners' control of their learning in these circumstances is not as complete as it is in the Educational Domain, but it is still significant. The larger the group, the greater the loss of individual control. Nonetheless, the result is an overall increased involvement in learning by the people who have access to the leave. For one thing, the arrangement of time involved in educational leave is likely to be more conducive to sustained learning than an hour or two less working time each week.

There can be no doubt that programs and arrangements of this kind will grow, consuming considerable sums of money and, more important, the time, attention, and will of increasing numbers of citizens. It therefore is important to grasp their fundamental character. Basically, in these programs the government does not determine the learning objectives to be reached except in the most general terms, nor does it determine or provide the methods of delivery of opportunities for learning. It delegates these things to agencies both inside and outside the formal educational system.

Until the mid-1970s the Canadian government relied more heavily than the government of any other industrial country on formal education providing agencies for the delivery of employment-related education and training (Organization for Economic Cooperation and Development, 1968). This meant that its programs were public and subject to the visibility and professional control common to all public education. Since that time, however, the federal government has shifted its financial support to a variety of private agencies, most notably employers (Dupre, 1973). This means that employers or related groups now control the objectives and the means of delivery of such learning. They make use of a wide range of both in-house and extramural resources, some of the latter drawn from the educational system.

Governments are delegating responsibility for the learning necessary to sustain a modern society to agencies outside the formal educational system on an unprecedented scale. The difference of some $16 billion in the two United States estimates of training program costs cited earlier indicates one common feature of these programs, the great difficulty in obtaining reliable information about their extent in terms either of expenditures or of numbers of participants. So far no government, to our knowledge, has evolved a systematic means of reporting on these activities, a curious lack when one considers what is at stake.

Similarly, few governments seem to have developed thorough or even adequate means of evaluating these programs or the organizations delegated to manage them. Clumsy as the formal educational system often was, the Canadian government, for one, is beginning to discover that in shifting resources away from traditional educational agencies it is losing a whole range of skills and services related to teacher selection, program development, and program evaluation. Governments in general are finding out, often through painful experience, that the encouragement of learning is a complex and subtle matter.

Aiding the Nonprofit Sector. There is an enormous literature on voluntary action. Most of it is North American, indicating the critical role of the volunteer phenomenon in North American society. It is interesting to note, however, the growing strength of such groups on the international scene, for example the astonishing success of voluntary groups of musicians in the production of the "Live-Aid" concert in the summer of 1985. This eight-hour rock concert, produced simultaneously from London and Philadelphia, was telecast to the world as a way of raising funds for Ethiopian famine relief. It reached a worldwide audience estimated at more than two billion and drew pledges totaling more than $100 million. It thus created a temporary global community as well as gaining unprecedented attention and money for its cause. The political implications of the learning involved are intriguing: citizens of individual nations, for however brief a period, learned how to act as citizens of the world. Popular music is not usually perceived as a vehicle for the development of political awareness, but there can be little doubt that it occurred in this case.

Satisfactory explanations for this and other volunteer groups' success are difficult to find, since voluntary behavior, like learning, usually is described and analyzed only in some particular context. The learning perspective, however, suggests that the source of the energy and commitment characteristic of volunteer action arises from the opportunity to learn, regardless of the specific objective pursued (National Advisory Committee on Voluntary Action, 1978; Carter, 1975).

One might think that there would be a significant difference between the means by which governments support the learning objectives of profit-making groups and those that they use to help nonprofit or voluntary groups, but a close examination reveals that this is not the case. By and large, governments provide direct and indirect support of learning connected with nonprofit groups in a manner similar to that used for commercial groups.

There have been longstanding differences between the United States and Canada in the procedures and attitudes that define the relationship between the countries' governments and nonprofit groups. The history of the United States, with its two major rebellions against centralized authority, has produced a widespread suspicion of government. Perhaps as a result of this, many volunteer groups in the United States have been extremely reluctant to accept or depend upon public funds. Though this reluctance has declined in recent years (for example, the country's public broadcasting system accepts government as well as private contributions), it has remained a powerful sentiment. In contrast, the more peaceful development of Canada and its relatively small population compared to its size have produced a less adversarial but extremely complex relationship between public and private interests in the maintenance of nongovernmental organizations and, therefore, in the support of learning connected with those organizations.

In all countries, nonprofit groups tend to fall into four categories: ideological groups, such as churches and political parties, in which membership is based on shared belief; advocacy groups, which are devoted to bringing about changes in the behavior of other members of the population (environmental protection groups, public health groups, and so on); service groups, such as "Meals on Wheels" or "Travellers' Aid"; and groups devoted to the support of a particular organization, such as theater support groups and hospital volunteer groups. Each of these categories tends to be treated somewhat differently by governments, although most of them, in most industrial societies, enjoy that most common of all forms of government support, relief from some forms of taxation. This benefits both the groups and their individual members. In North America, for example, churches have long enjoyed freedom from property tax, and all nonprofit organizations are exempted from payment of income tax. The next most common government benefit, granted to at least some nonprofit organizations, is permission for donors to exempt contributions to such organizations from their own taxable income, which obviously encourages contributions to those organizations. The amount of income foregone by governments through granting of tax-relief benefits to nonprofit organizations is considerable. In Canada it amounts to between approximately $800 million and $1 billion a year.

Canadian nonprofit organizations must apply to the federal government (specifically to Revenue Canada, since the legal provision involved is a section of the Income Tax Act) and be registered in order for their contributors to be able to deduct donations from taxable income. The law provides few guidelines for the officials who must decide whether to accept or reject each application. If an organization's application is refused, the group's only recourse is appeal to the courts, a lengthy and expensive process that is beyond the means of most volunteer organizations. This procedure thus places considerable control over the development of such organizations, especially national ones, in government hands. About 4,500 applications for registration are made each year, of which about 80 percent are accepted (Federal Court of Appeal, 1982, 1985). The vagueness of the criteria for acceptance, as well as the grounds on which some organizations (particularly advocacy organizations) have been refused registration or deprived of registration gained earlier, has caused increasing numbers of these organizations to resort to lawsuits. Such friction probably will continue to grow.

Nonprofit groups ask their supporters to donate money, time, or both. Volunteers' time (and energy, skill, attention, loyalty, and so on) is used directly in pursuit of the group's objectives; their money helps the group by, among other things, allowing it to hire a certain number of full-time salaried workers. Balancing the two resources of time and money has created a dilemma for many nonprofit organizations. On one hand, the more sophisticated and specialized a group and its objectives are, the more likely the group is to become impatient with most volunteer labor and to prefer to spend money to hire workers with special skills. On the other hand, the more specialized and inscrutable an organization is perceived as being and the less interested it appears to be in its volunteers, the less likely people are to support it.

Most people who join volunteer organizations are seeking a chance to learn and to do something significant. Even though one may receive organizational newsletters or the like in return for donations, one can learn rather little just by giving money. Organizations that reject the donation of volunteers' time, therefore, are likely to lose their money as well. When people have a choice, as they do with volunteer organizations, they increasingly refuse to support groups that do not in turn support and nurture their individual learning. This behavior provides a lesson for the future that governments and educational institutions as well as leaders of nonprofit organizations would do well to heed.

The time versus money dilemma is particularly acute for volunteer organizations in Canada at the moment. Large numbers of these organizations are submitting to some degree of government control in an attempt to gain tax-exempt status and thus increase donations, with little appreciation of the grounds on which that control is exercised and little protection against arbitrary exercise of government power. Although groups of any size may apply for the privilege of offering tax exemption for donations, they must be willing and able to go through the legal procedures of incorporation and application for charitable status in order to do so. Many small community and neighborhood organizations cannot afford to make their way through this time-consuming and costly legal labyrinth. It is all too clear, therefore, that only large organizations really benefit from this approach to winning donations when it succeeds, and only they, or groups of smaller organizations acting together, can afford the expense of legal appeals when it fails. These large organizations thus are the only ones that can offer tax relief to the individual, but they are also the ones most likely to be professionalized and indifferent to the personal contributions of volunteers.

Some have argued that the special status system for Canadian volunteer organizations should be eliminated, thus removing the advantages currently enjoyed by large organizations and wealthy donors. Such a step certainly would reduce government influence on these organizations, and perhaps Canada is sufficiently developed to afford it now. This move might open the door to a substantial increase in voluntarism and in the vigor and variety of volunteer organizations. On the other hand, it might produce a loss of financial support that could cause volunteer organizations to become even more dependent upon government grants than they are at present, thus increasing government influence. If the present system is maintained, both greater clarity concerning grounds for tax-exempt status and easier access to appeal in case of rejection or removal of that preferred status need to be established.

Governments often use nonprofit groups to provide services that can be managed best by a mixture of paid and volunteer labor, a mixture that is quite impossible for governments themselves to provide. This delegation is a relatively new phenomenon, dating back only about twenty years. Before the late 1960s, private groups usually identified what they saw as inadequacies in the greater society, showed (or attempted to show) how these might be removed, and then persuaded the government to assume responsibility for making the proposed changes. At about that time, however, it became clear to governments and citizens alike that public administration simply was not equipped to remedy certain kinds of social lacks. Volunteer organizations such as the "Big Brothers," on the other hand, could provide the sort of personalized attention needed by, in this case, young boys from broken or disturbed homes.

There may never be complete agreement on what government's relationship to volunteer groups should be, but we urge that it always be weighted in favor of opportunities for learning. Large public and private bureaucracies seem to provide little opportunity for releasing the potential of individual learning, whereas the combination of government financial power and voluntary initiative and commitment, when properly managed, appear to maximize that potential for the benefit of both the individual and the community.

Delegating Learning Programs. We have seen that governments in recent years have often delegated at least part of the responsibility for meeting citizens' learning needs to for-profit or nonprofit groups outside the educational system. Such delegation has tended to be concentrated in areas related to health, welfare, the arts, athletics and amateur sports, and, as we have described, employment.

One example of a large-scale delegated program was the training support program arranged between the Canadian government and a number of labor organizations beginning in 1970.

The organizations had argued for some years that the government should pay for training workers in a variety of skills that were needed to manage the labor movement and that the formal educational system, for the most part, had been both indifferent to their special needs and incompetent to meet them. In response to these complaints, the government began a series of annual grants to labor organizations to pay for increased training programs for their members. By doing this the government in effect agreed that the skills being learned by the members and officers of the labor organizations were beneficial to the society as a whole and thereby worthy of public support. The labor training program was evaluated twice in its first five-year period, and the evaluation concluded that, on the whole, the government's investment had more than justified itself in terms of increased opportunities for members to take part in training programs, the quality of new teaching materials and resources, and the breadth of topics addressed (Thomas, Abbey, and Mac-Keracher, 1982). Similar support for labor programs has been provided on a substantial scale by European governments, particularly those of Britain and Scandinavia.

The Canadian government's decision to fund the labor education program seems to have been based on two principles. The first was that the skills involved in managing labor organizations were of sufficient value to the society to warrant public support. This belief was based on the government's experience in trying to administer a turbulent economy on the basis of cooperation between government, labor, and business, during which it had discovered that there were very few labor representatives who had the negotiating abilities and other skills needed for such complex cooperation. The government's underlying policy, therefore, could not be carried out unless there was a substantial increase in trained labor representatives. Here was a clear case of needing to pay existing pipers to learn a new tune.

The second principle involved in the government's decision is perhaps even more important. The government concluded that the labor organizations themselves, rather than educational providing agencies, were the best ones to help people learn the desired skills. The labor organizations, after all, had developed these skills, understood their application, and could be counted on to make the quickest and most efficient use of people who acquired them. The government's greatest concern was not how the skills were taught but the assurance that they were learned. This latter principle seems to be becoming the basis for increasing numbers of government-sponsored learning programs everywhere.

In programs of this sort, the government is delegating the identification of learning needs, both individual and collective, to organizations not explicitly designed for the purpose of education. Such programs have both advantages and disadvantages. To begin with, they obviously require that a person have some relationship with the source of learning support before he or she can gain access to the program. In other words, the person must be either employee or member before translating himself or herself into learner. In educational institutions, by contrast, no prior relationship is required before one becomes a student; the role is open to all, at least theoretically, on the basis of age in the case of elementary and (usually) secondary education and on the basis of intellectual ability at postsecondary levels.

We have already commented on the powerful role that a sense of membership plays in motivating people to learn. Where such membership is required for access to learning opportunities, the commitment to group-specified learning objectives and to the activity of learning itself is apt to be very high. However, when a government delegates the provision of learning opportunities to noneducational organizations on a large scale, it risks excluding potential learners who, for one reason or another, do not enjoy the required relationship with the organizations. The unemployed, for example, usually cannot take advantage of programs provided by either employers or labor organizations. Similarly, many unemployed women ("just housewives") may be important members of their families, but that membership brings them little in the way of public or private support for learning. Unemployed people (except members of the latter group who already have enjoyed success as students in their early education) also are unlikely to be conventional students. Lack of access to learning opportunities thus is likely to have a major impact on the lives of at least two groups of citizens and probably of many more.

"Lack of access," incidentally, can be a subtle matter. Even though increasing numbers of women are employees (Skill Development Leave Task Force, 1983) and thus technically have access to employee training programs, the records indicate that as a group they participate much less than men in such programs. Apparently women often do not perceive employment training to be important enough to their careers to be worth the extra demands it makes on them, such as the demand to give up time that otherwise could be spent at home with the family. Many women also lack confidence in their ability to complete such programs. Worse still, employers and fellow male employees often share the view that training programs are not relevant or necessary for women, so women employees are not recruited for the programs and may not know of their existence. All of these factors are changing, largely because employers are learning that they cannot do without the potential that women employees present, but the process is slow, too slow.

A second characteristic of learning programs delegated to noneducational organizations is that these organizations often can provide little or none of the protection that allows conventional students to make safely the mistakes that learning requires. For one thing, students eventually graduate and leave the environment where they may have failed several times before they succeeded, but learners in the workplace and related settings lack comparable freedom to escape the consequences of their failures, since normally they want to continue to be employed at the same place of business. For another, on-the-job learning often is closely related to action and therefore to affecting the real world. Errors may be irrecoverable and failures permanent.

To be sure, businesses and other noneducational organizations can build some protection into their learning programs by providing their own forms of segregation for learners and by offering simulations that allow experimentation without disastrous results. The now-famous "Harvard Case Method" for teaching students of business is one example of a program that uses simulation (case studies, in this instance). Such programs are likely to become increasingly widespread. The escape afforded to conventional students by graduation, however, remains unavailable to employee-learners, except perhaps in the largest organizations, in which, say, a transfer to a different branch or department might be possible.

Another interesting contrast between learning programs outside and inside the formal educational system occurs in attitudes toward novelty and evaluation. In the Educational Domain, change in curriculum is slow and judicious; indeed, a primary objective of educational systems often seems to be that such change not be noticeable at all. In the Learning Domain, by contrast, change is welcomed, in fact demanded. There the feeling is that if your program resembles the program of two years ago, you are not doing your job. Similarly, in the Educational Domain it is the student who is evaluated (passed or failed). Only if an unusual number of students pass or fail is the program evaluated, and only after that the teacher. In the Learning Domain, however, the teacher and the program are the first to be evaluated and, if necessary, changed if students do not learn.

It is little wonder that participants in these two worlds, both concerned with learning, have so little understanding of each other. Both teachers and learners expect and display different behavior in each of these domains. Furthermore, differences in the management of learning between the Learning Domain and the Educational Domain are significant, inescapable, and desirable. In the past our societies have depended on the Learning Domain for the bulk of adult learning, but currently, as adult participation in formal programs both inside and outside conventional educational institutions steadily increases, learners often are caught between the two approaches.

The present-day public support of learning in the Learning Domain is widespread but only occasionally visible. The extent of it can be glimpsed by examining the daily schedules displayed by any modern hotel or large motel during the working week and discovering how many of the events listed are associated with learning. We know of no available figures, but we would guess that 60 to 70 percent of such events fit into this category. These schedules and similar documents show that everywhere small groups of people, sponsored by a variety of public and private organizations, are devoting time and effort to learning improved sales techniques, better supervisory skills, methods for using new technological devices, or how to organize and run a meeting, to name just a few of the possibilities.

The relative invisibility of these Learning Domain activities has two kinds of consequences. First, as noted earlier, if a person lacks access to the specialized networks in which the activities occur, he or she will have no way even to know of these learning opportunities' existence, let alone take advantage of them. If the activities are publicly supported, however, citizens have some right and even some responsibility to know about them. The second consequence is that present systems of data collection concerning "education" in most industrial societies are, by their nature, incapable of reporting accurately about learning in this context. We may believe that we know approximately what our children and young people are being taught, but we have little or no idea what the adult population is learning. To be ignorant of that is to deny ourselves the most important of all information about the present and future of our society. We need to create some type of public agency, independent of government, whose job is to report annually on the learning activities of all of a country's citizens. Information of that kind is not difficult to gather (Thomas, MacKeracher, MacNeil, and Selman, 1982; Tough, 1978), and its availability to governments, groups, and individual citizens would be indispensable.

Providing Learning Resources. In response to pressure from groups who claim to have identified learning needs of value to the whole society, governments often establish specific resources to help people meet those needs. These resources can be used freely by the public. The classic example of such a resource is the public library, which began to become widespread in industrial societies toward the end of the nineteenth century and became as conventional a resource as the public school system by the middle of the twentieth. Additional educational resources that may be supported by governments include art

galleries, museums, parks, science and technology centers, plane-
taria, and wilderness reserves. Of a slightly different order, but
still part of learning resources, are theater and opera companies, symphony orchestras and other music groups, and agencies of television production and broadcasting. These latter
represent a slight overlap of the Learning and Educational domains. For the most part these resources are supported by a
mixture of government funds and private contributions.

It is important to note that all of the organizations just
mentioned are resources for learning, not sources of teaching,
although almost all of them, understandably, exhibit an "itch
to teach" and maintain some form of instruction, usually associated with an attempt to increase membership. In Canada,
many of these organizations, such as the Royal Ontario Museum,
began as part of teaching and research institutions.

Obviously these resources will not appeal, or apply to
everyone, since, among other things, they are biased by the
dominant interests of the societies in which they have developed.
Public libraries, for example, were established to make first information and then entertainment available in printed form in
societies in which print had become the predominant form of
communication. Therefore, despite their inclusion of discussion
programs, video and audio tape rental, storytelling hours for
children, and so on, public libraries remain a resource chiefly
for the kind of information that print provides.

The spectrum of senses taken seriously as vehicles for
learning seems to be broadening slowly, however. The rise of
film, radio, and television has produced new support (both public
and private) for theater, symphony, opera, and the like. Access to radio material remains primitive (some famous old radio shows have been reissued on commercially available audio
tapes, but not many), and video rental shops at present are
usually commercial ventures, like the private lending libraries
of the nineteenth century, but it is likely that access to these
media, too, soon will be provided at public expense. Recent support in North America for resources involving nonprint communications media suggest both the lessening of the grip that
print once exercised on North American society and the steadily growing influence of the new media.

Other learning resources are provided for the for-profit sector, partly as low-interest loans and partly as technical resource centers, such as the Technology Centers in the province of Ontario and sources of sales and export advice provided by the Canadian government. Historically, one of the most important of such government-supported learning resources in both Canada and the United States was "agricultural extension," which provided learning resources of all kinds to the once dominant farmer. The present difficulties in making learning resources available to the small business owner suggest that some modified and updated version of agricultural extension may be desirable. A regional College of Applied Arts and Technology in northwestern Ontario has been experimenting with the development of such a service. Through regional offices it offers advice and information to help owners of small businesses solve problems of management, accounting, government regulations, and other common difficulties. Personnel attached to these offices resemble the traditional agricultural "county agents," who, in the first half of this century, discovered that farmers needed as much help in handling the business aspect of their farms as they did in dealing with the technical problems of agriculture.

A third significant area of publicly supported learning resources involves what is commonly called "culture." In popular usage this term usually has meant materials and activities of a relatively sophisticated nature, participated in by elite minorities of various kinds. However, the introduction of new media, which require either active (as in the case of broadcasting, which must be licensed following a public review process) or passive (as in the case of film, which must not violate obscenity laws) government approval, seems to be changing this interpretation. The millions of young people who participate in the "culture" of rock music, for example, can hardly be described as a sophisticated minority. The same is true of audiences for films and television, despite the fact that they are responding to types of aural and visual stimulation that in the past have been associated with "culture." Contemporary musical recordings and rock videos show where today's real poets and social critics are. The fact that many radio stations are virtually controlled by the musical tastes of young audiences also suggests something of the new power and influence in what used to be regarded as a marginal activity. A great deal of attention is being paid to these new forms of expression, and a great deal of learning is the result. "Culture," formerly often ignored or regarded as of benefit to only a few, is becoming the pivot of our societies and our futures.

The lessons of the past thirty years in regard to the social or collective dimensions of the management of learning have been very clear. Governments can permit or, to a lesser and less successful extent, forbid learning through law, but their most important modern role is in the encouragement of support of learning in the Learning Domain through such techniques as the provision of learning resources (such as libraries, museums, and broadcasting outlets) and the more explicit cosponsorship of specialized programs such as those for training employees.

Government activity, especially support, in the Learning Domain has been limited until recently, however, by the assumption that the learning that occurred in the Educational Domain — that is, learning directed by the state — was the only learning that really mattered. In the following chapter we will discuss the characteristics and the limits of the Educational Domain from the perspective of the overall learning taking place in society. Such an examination is intended to shed new light on the relationship between the Learning and the Educational domains and to indicate why neither one can function in modern society without a full realization of the potential and limits of the other.

6

The Limits of
Formal Education

In addition to permitting, forbidding, and encouraging learning, governments can respond to their citizens' learning potential by directing learning through what is known universally as "formal education." As we have described in Chapter Two and elsewhere, confidence in this form of learning management was also universal during the first half of this century but has come to be just as widely questioned during recent years. H. G. Wells's famous statement in favor of education, "History is a race between education and catastrophe," which appeared in a book published in 1920, could be said to mark the beginning of this era of confidence. G. Counts's article, "Dare the Schools Build a New Social Order?" first published in 1932, could be said to mark the beginning of the end of it.

During most of this century, governments have translated the bulk of their citizens' identified learning needs into educational ones, thus causing the citizens to enter what we have called the Educational Domain in an attempt to satisfy those needs. Governments have chosen the direction of learning through the formal educational system as their preferred form of learning management because this approach offers the promise of a greater degree of control in producing specific learning outcomes than would be possible if learning needs were met in the Learning Domain. The appearance of control comes from students'

development of visible (and to some degree measurable and cer-
tifiable) knowledge, skills, and attitudes and from the fact that
the means of that development is also visible, that is, amenable
to public (government) inspection.

In many ways the formal educational system has served
Western industrial societies well. As a socializing agency for the
young, it has provided a powerful source of stability for societies faced with increasingly rapid technological change. In addition, it has made possible massive but reasonably orderly shifts
in the composition of populations within nation-states and, in
the case of immigrant societies, between them. It has provided
a common experience for millions of young people that offered
some glimpse, first of other children and other ways of life, and
then of other aspirations and possibilities besides those provided
by their parents.

Nonetheless, the formal educational system has many
flaws, which its critics have been pointing out with increasing
emphasis. It clearly has not provided the expected equality of
opportunity for all of society's children, for one thing. The conclusion seems inescapable that rich communities and countries
maintain rich schools, not the reverse. While this failure to provide equal opportunity is most dramatic in regard to certain
racial groups, such as blacks in the United States and Native
Americans in both the United States and Canada, its effects can
be seen in poor families regardless of race: education has failed
to break the cycle of poverty that frequently continues in such
families from generation to generation (Kaplan, 1986; Brown,
1968).

This chapter will examine the flaws and contradictions
within the formal educational system and the historical factors
that have caused these flaws to develop. Each of the elements
of formal education — its youthful target population, its physical environment, books, teachers, and certification — has contributed to the system's contradictions. Together these elements
comprise the "form" in formal education. As we argued in our
analysis of the student role and lifestyle in Chapter Three, it
is this form that remains in the mind long after details of mathe-
matical tables and dates from history have been forgotten. The

form rather than the content of formal education, therefore, is the most important aspect to study from the perspective of learning management. This chapter will examine the familiar elements of the educational system from this somewhat unfamiliar but revealing perspective.

The Politics of Education

When a government attempts to direct learning through formal education, it must follow a number of steps and make a number of decisions. First, as with other government activities, goals must be determined through public debate. Then the target population must be identified; means for carrying out the activity must be devised, including incentives to participate; places where instruction is to be conducted must be built; materials and programs must be prepared; a special body of managers, in this case called teachers, must be trained and employed; a plan for advancing through the system, which includes several different kinds of providing agencies, must be devised; and a method of certifying successful completion of stages of advancement or other objectives must be established. Regardless of the instructional goals and methods chosen, the types of decisions related to the direction of learning are essentially the same.

Today, government decisions about any part of the educational process almost invariably have a political element. The North American decision to entrust the education of children and youth to local authorities responsible to an electorate means that debate about education is a continuous feature of local politics. The more advanced levels of education in these societies, such as colleges and universities, resemble the more centralized European and Asian systems. They also spark debate, but the political mechanisms involved are less obvious.

As educational systems have become more inclusive, they have come to be perceived by parents (correctly, at least in Canada) as the chief ladders of mobility for their children (Podoluk, 1968); by employers as the chief source of trained employees; and by politicians and community leaders as the foundation of civil order and national stability. No other social agency has been expected to carry so many burdens or has been given such close attention by so many citizens.

Until recently, most citizens' relationship to the schools arose from the fact that they were parents. Today, however, as people (at least in the industrial nations) have fewer children, citizens are becoming more likely to be concerned with schools because they are students or potential students. The political consequences of this development are only beginning to emerge.

As educational systems have grown larger, more complex, and more professionalized, their procedures and methods of operation have become more inscrutable not only to the average citizen but even to their students. The traditional student of the educational systems that dominated this century needed to know only three things in order to enter the system: the fact that attendance was legally required, the hours and months during which attendance was expected, and the location of the school. Once the student was inside the school, all behavior was determined; one went where one was told to go. Today, however, entering and moving about in an educational system have become much more confusing, both physically and procedurally. The physical maze of buildings on an average university or secondary school campus is matched only by the bureaucratic maze of forms and procedures that face the new or would-be student, especially one who seeks to enter the system at something other than its traditional entry points. The growth of educational counseling and "brokering" services and the increase in public information about education (Fournier, 1982) attest both to the complexity of gaining access to educational systems and to the increased demand from nontraditional would-be students for help in doing so.

Elements of the Formal Educational System

The chief elements that comprise the "form" of formal education are the target population, the physical environment, books, teachers, and certification. All of these elements have contributed to both the strengths and the weaknesses of the present-day educational system. These elements' nature and effect on learning have their roots in the elements' historical development. Our understanding of their significance, therefore, can be increased by examining their history.

Target Population. Some of the confusion in today's educational system has arisen from the fact that the system's target population is changing. From the turn of the century until recently, nations agreed that the target population for education should consist largely of children and young people, up to some cutoff point. Debate focused mostly on whether all children or just some should have the benefits of publicly supported education and for how many years. (The profound idea of the "common school" [Cremin, 1951; Cremin, 1961] for the young as the great equalizer of social opportunity was a peculiarly American invention, though it spread to other countries as the century passed.) This choice of target population was related to the belief that only children were capable of significant learning. Most Canadians, for example, have continued to believe that only children can learn a language (including a second language) properly (Penfield, 1959), even though research strongly suggests that this is not true.

In addition to agreeing on the target population for education, people in most parts of the world came to agree that all of a country's adult citizens should be collectively responsible for the education of all of its children and that public education therefore should be financed by public taxation. This agreement was not achieved easily by any means, but acceptance of financing education through taxation was aided immeasurably by a rising middle class that recognized that their children's success would depend almost entirely upon the acquisition of knowledge and skills that could be provided only by public education. Now that the target population for formal education is changing from youth only to a mixture of young people and adults, the idea that all education should be paid for by public money is being challenged.

Physical Environment. The way in which instruction is delivered is another important aspect of the means by which education is provided. Despite some ideas about one-to-one teaching within formal systems, traditionally represented by the universities of Oxford and Cambridge, governments and most providing agencies usually have decided that instruction must be conducted in groups. Since learning is solely individual in character, tension between the means and the ends of education thus has become inescapable.

If instruction is to be delivered to groups, it follows logically that those groups must be put somewhere. In early North America they were put in the "schoolhouse," architecturally a combination of simple chapel and even simpler domestic dwelling. In Europe the school building was apt to be a converted church or guildhall; in Asia, it was likely to be an adjunct to a temple. In later years, large numbers of relatively simple buildings were used to make schools for young children so that the children could remain close to home. Since closeness to home was less important for older children and a need for specialized facilities was more so, schools for youth ("high" or secondary schools) tended to involve fewer but more complex buildings arranged in clusters, somewhat resembling factories.

The physical environment of universities appears to have ecclesiastic or imperial roots, but no clear educational style of architecture seems to have emerged. The resulting diversity surely has had its effects on university students. It is impossible to believe that students at a university physically integrated into the middle of a busy city, such as the universities of London, Paris, or Chicago, can have the same experience in learning who they are or what knowledge is as the students of relatively isolated, self-contained universities such as the universities of Wisconsin, Maryland, or British Columbia, let alone a place like Simon Fraser University in Vancouver, Canada, with its unified design and commanding location on a mountaintop that on a clear day seems to echo Abelard's invocation to his students: "Ye are not men, ye are Gods."

Whatever their exteriors, the internal character of spaces dedicated to education are everywhere the same: the classroom, the laboratory, the auditorium, the library, the gymnasium. These are the architectural boundaries of student life, and they have been so for a thousand years and more. Even during the radical educational experimentation of the 1970s they were never left far behind. In particular, the "classroom" lies at the center of the enterprise, a sanctuary for both teacher and student. Even when adults are taught in noneducational settings such as industry, the armed services, or prisons, the classroom remains the preferred location for instruction.

A final factor of education's physical environment is transportation. If schools are so far from students' homes that students cannot walk to school, the students must be carried there. In the past three decades demands for efficiency everywhere, abetted by demands for racially integrated schooling especially in the United States, have led to centralization of schools and extensive "busing," especially for rural children. There is probably no more ubiquitous symbol of education in North America than the school bus, shaped and colored like an oversize bumblebee. The length of time spent by many children on these buses, up to two hours every day, suggests that some powerful learning must take place on the bus itself, though so far as we know, no one has yet seen fit to record and interpret it.

Books. The development of large-scale formal systems of education was shaped by the printed word—the book—more than by any other single factor (McLuhan, 1969; Steinberg, 1974). Printed matter was most dramatically important in education in North America and other immigrant societies. Books were the predominant, sometimes the only, cultural artifacts that settlers carried with them. The book thus became the primary cultural building block for new communities and civilizations that lacked the identity and cohesion provided by the presence of a familiar countryside and architectural reminders of shared heritage. In emerging nation-states, books provided the chief means of spreading common information over vast distances (geographical, cultural, or both). By being supplied with identical books, people believed, children from extremely disparate backgrounds could be turned into sufficiently identical citizens.

Educational program decisions that in earlier times had

been based on the availability of competent teachers came to
be based instead on the availability of suitable books. Books,
in turn, were developed especially for school use. These so-called
textbooks covered an amount of material that was deemed appropriate for teaching during a fixed school period to an "average" class. The unit of the curriculum was (and to a great degree
remains) the book, and movement through the school system
came to be symbolized primarily by passage through a series
of books. As late as the 1930s, the first three years of elementary school in Ontario were formally called Book I, Book II,
and Book III. Edgerton Ryerson, the founder of public education in that province, is said to have boasted that he could sit
in his office in the Parliament Buildings and know at any moment which page of his "reader" every child in the province was
turning.

Given the book's controlling role in education, it was not
surprising that extracting information from the printed word
(reading) and delivering it through the written word (writing)
became the predominant skills both conveyed and demanded
by educational systems. Probably no other human abilities have
been the focus of so much time, attention, and argument (for
example, Flesch, 1955; Waples, Berelson, and Bradshaw, 1940;
Scribner and Cole, 1981). Other abilities, such as calculating,
drawing, or playing a musical instrument, were regarded as re-
quiring possession of a special talent, so some tolerance was
granted to those who were inept at them. Everyone, however,
was expected to master reading and writing; to be inept at these
was to fail the system.

As other media of communication, such as radio (speech
and music), film (speech, movement, design, music), and television, have increasingly penetrated homes and psyches in recent years, many of the societal supports for reading and writing have disappeared, and the biases of the schools toward these
skills have begun to seem inappropriate to some. Educational
programs have broadened sufficiently to provide some rewards
for other skills, but progress is slow and frictions remain. In
fact, the spreading use of personal computers, which combine
the printed word with the speed and flexibility commonly as-

sociated with oral communications, has provided new support for demands for literacy. The designation by UNESCO of 1990 as "International Literacy Year" shows a universal concern about literacy and its lack, especially among adults.

There is little indication so far of any major change in the traditional relationships among student, book, and teacher. Books are the distillation of what someone else has learned. Teachers already know it. The intent of the present system is that students will learn this material with as little change as possible in the knowledge itself. In essence that is what the direction of learning has meant. To change these relationships would alter the educational system dramatically.

Teachers. Only in discussing the elements of the educational system as it has existed in the past century could one deal with teachers and teaching last. Prior to the widespread utilization of the printed book that occurred during that time, the availability of the teacher always took precedence over the establishment of the school.

One effect of our profound commitment to formal education is the widespread belief that teaching and learning are inseparable. This sometimes amounts to a sort of educational totalitarianism, represented in the maxim, "If it hasn't been taught, it isn't worth knowing." In fact, however, learning always outstrips teaching, as has become increasingly clear in our "information age." Furthermore, learning can and does take place without teaching, but teaching, by definition, cannot take place without learning, although behavior associated with the intention to teach may exist when little or no learning takes place.

Conflicting views of teaching and learning are further complicated by the variety of uses of the two terms. For example, people often report that they have been "taught" something by someone but actually mean that they have learned from a powerful example of particular behavior. The source of that behavior is often unaware of or indifferent to the fact that he or she has provided a stimulus to learning. This situation is called "teaching" mainly because of the belief that all significant learning must result from teaching. It is nonetheless quite different from teaching in school, which is deliberate and systematic. In fact, it is an example of learning that does not result from teaching.

A glance at the history of education suggests that there have been two principal types of teachers. In the first group we find the prophets, the moralists, the intellectual leaders. These people are committed to a certain set of ideas, standard of behavior, or vision of the world that their own behavior exemplifies, and they set out to share their ideas with the rest of humankind. "I am the way" is the message of every prophet. Many martyrs are to be found in this group, since their views are usually at odds with the status quo and they cannot be deflected from their mission.

The other type of teacher is a person who can teach a variety of skills or ideas without necessarily being personally identified with any of them. At best, such a person is committed to teaching itself (or perhaps to teaching some particular group, such as children or immigrants). Plato distrusted such teachers, naming them "sophists," but modern educational systems could not exist without them. To be sure, as one proceeds upwards in the educational system, more specialization in knowledge and more personal identification with particular learning outcomes can be found. The university professor, devoted to a combination of teaching and research, is perhaps the nearest one comes to the first kind of teacher in formal educational systems. That may be the reason why the contemporary university is so uneasy a part of an educational system dominated by the other type of teacher.

The reason why the second type of teacher fits contemporary educational systems better than the first is clear. The architects of these systems believed passionately in the need for education for all children and in the primacy of the book as the basis of instruction. They perceived teachers as hardly more than group managers and mediators between books and pupils. Only after laws compelling school attendance were passed, school buildings were found or constructed, and books in suitably graduated form were provided was a search for a teacher conducted. If a fully trained teacher could not be found, then a partly trained or untrained teacher was appointed.

Few, if any, schools in North America (or in any of the other modern Western-style educational systems) have been closed because of the absence of a fully trained teacher. Many teachers in the first half of the century pursued their training after they had been appointed; indeed, many North American universities made their first provisions for part-time students in order to allow for the education of employed teachers. Until recently, university activities in the summer have been virtually synonymous with teacher training.

With the status of the teaching profession lodged somewhere between traditional respect for the teacher (usually the first type of teacher) and the reality of employment in a relatively low-paying job with poor chances for advancement, teaching has tended to attract people from less well-off families. To be sure, as teachers have become more numerous and more highly trained, they have come to play a more professional and independent role in schools and classrooms. Nevertheless, with respect to choice of program materials, time allotment, and procedures, it is evident to both students and the public that the teacher is almost as externally controlled as the student. This external control is the chief reason for the limitations on learning outcomes that seem to pervade modern educational systems. A learner must truly "own" his or her learning in order for that learning to succeed. In school, however, there is always the sense that someone else owned it first and perhaps still does.

In many respects the contemporary teacher is even more a product of the educational system than the student. The happiest and most productive teachers often appear to be those who teach elective subjects such as music, art, or athletics — subjects that students take only if they wish to. The experience of these teachers thus approximates the experience of the teacher of courses for adults, in which most participation is voluntary. Even in these cases, however, the system dominates their professional lives.

Certification. It is a curious fact that the development of formal education in its present character robbed the traditional terms for progress in learning of their meaning. The words *gradu-*

ation and *degree,* which imply a portion of something, originally were intended to signify not termination or completion, as they do today, but merely "punctuation" in a lifelong sequence of learning. The change is particularly clear in the use of the American term *commencement,* which literally means a beginning (presumably the beginning of "real life" in the world of work) but today is usually associated with the completion of secondary school. The suggestion of the latter usage is that education, school, and, by inference, learning must cease at the point when real life begins. Common phrases such as "when you have finished school" and "completing your education" also reflect the idea that formal education (and, by implication, learning) is expected to be completed at some fixed point in time. Until recently this belief was reflected in widespread practices that made reentry into the educational system both extremely difficult and highly unlikely, particularly if exit had occurred somewhere other than at a few critical points such as the end of secondary school or college. It was the certifying power of the educational system, represented by school certificates, diplomas, and degrees, that changed the meaning of the original proportionate terms. Their former meaning is now slowly being restored, however, as "continuing education" becomes a reality for more and more people (Department of Adult Education, Ontario Institute for Studies in Education, 1981).

We have already observed that during all of the experimentation with the role of the student that took place during the 1960s and 1970s, one factor that did not vary was the right of the educational authority to make a final evaluation of the student's achievement. The reasons for the preservation of that right are clear enough. Certification is a responsibility both to the student and to the society at large. It is, in effect, a franchise granted by governments to selected providing agencies. In Canada, as in most other countries, these agencies are entirely public in character; that is, they have been created expressly for the purpose of exercising the franchise and providing the means to achieve certification. They are financed almost entirely from the public purse. To be sure, some private institutions with the right to certify are to be found at all levels of education, particularly at the university level in the United States, and universities in the eastern and central regions of Canada were private agencies until the middle of this century.

The certificate or degree granted by these educational institutions not only informs the student of his or her abilities as determined by the agency; it also informs society. Such certification has become more and more accepted, indeed required, by employers as the century has progressed. Educational agencies thus have become more and more the exclusive gateways to income, status, and advancement. In addition, as the rate of technological innovation has increased, new demands for certification have been directed to adults past the conventional age of participation in formal education. Certification has become necessary not only as a means of advancement but as a means of maintaining a position already reached. The pressure on the providing agencies to make programs leading to certification more accessible to nonconventional students has increased commensurately. As a result, providing agencies have both extended their traditional programs and experimented with different means of granting various certificates and degrees.

Changing the experiences that lead to certification undeniably alters what the certified person knows and can do and thus changes the meaning of the certification. Questions have been raised, therefore, about the quality of certificates obtained from experimental programs as compared to that of certificates from traditional ones (Gould, 1974). A considerable informal system of distinguishing between similar certificates achieved in different societies has grown up, and some distinction also is made among certificates from different providing agencies. The practice of attaching the name of a particular agency to the certificate, as in the case of university degrees, seems to be on the increase. Learning may be a seamless robe, but education certainly is not.

Unfortunately, certification by the formal education system stimulates and rewards only a limited range of learning objectives. Imposing these same limits on the basis for employment and promotion within the society as a whole can only curtail that society's diversity and resilience. Furthermore, the

knowledge and skill whose acquisition is attested to by the certification required to gain entry to a particular job often are
related only marginally to the performance of that job.

In most countries during the past century, formal educational agencies have provided certain programs for people (almost invariably adults) who wished to learn what they provided
but lacked the qualifications or the interest to enroll in a formal
"credit" program (Blyth, 1976; Kidd, 1961; Curti, 1949). Sometimes such activities have been originated by highly motivated
individuals acting more or less on their own. At other times,
special agencies, such as the American "land-grant" universities and community colleges, have been established to provide
them. In mainstream educational agencies at least, such programs for the most part have been perceived as marginal and
indeed have operated under a constant threat of elimination
despite their provision of revenue, allowance for experimentation, and drawing to the agency of an additional and perhaps
crucial segment of the population. Anything that falls outside
of educational institutions' principal business of certification
receives similar treatment.

Achievement of a proper balance between an individual's
freedom to learn and society's need to judge and control is as
vital as it is difficult. Many people see certification as necessary
to maintain standards of knowledge and competence. Overem-
phasis on formal certification, however, can lead to the creation of an "education society," a poor and limited substitute for
a "learning society" based on the maximization of individual
learning capabilities.

Contradictions in the Educational Domain

As the century has progressed, formal educational systems have developed internal contradictions that no amount of
adjustment or tinkering seems able to resolve. The first is that
they are "front-end loaded": that is, they concentrate on preparation for action and for life. To the extent that these systems
deal with the part of the population that is at the "front end"
of life (children and youth), this bias seems neither surprising

nor inappropriate, provided that the experience with learning is not regarded as terminal by either the agencies or the students. The bias does become inappropriate, however, when the systems are considered, as they should be, as agencies for providing continuing education, accessible to students of any age and any level of achievement. Far from needing preparation for life, an increasing number of today's students have been taking an active part in life before entering the system. All present trends suggest that the increase in such students will continue.

Even though most formal educational systems now admit growing numbers of adult students, the idea of "preparation" remains strong in the materials and teaching used. This can lead to an uneasy kind of fiction with respect to the meaning and utility of courses of instruction. The older student is forced to accept the incongruous pretense that only when a program of courses is completed will he or she be recognized by the providing agency and the society as being competent in any part of the skills and knowledge arising from the program. This can lead to frustration and discouragement for older students, with consequent loss to the society.

The instructional problem endemic to the view of education as "preparation" is that the subject matter's claim to relevance rests on the authority of the provider rather than on the previous experience of the learner. The instruction presents answers to questions that supposedly have not yet appeared in the experience of the learner, and the learner therefore must take the relevance of both the questions and the answers on faith. This situation stands in sharp contrast to that in the Learning Domain, in which learning follows confrontation with a problem rather than preceding it. This issue affects not only adults forced to deal with a system designed for children but also adolescents, many of whom are already assuming or being invested with adult responsibilities. Older students, by their very presence in formal systems, are already bringing about changes in this bias, but some radical rethinking and reorganization of programs to make them more appropriate for certain ages and circumstances is likely to be necessary. It could be said that the measure of the success of any educational program is the degree to which its graduates continue to engage in self-directed learning, whether inside or outside the formal educational system.

Linked to this contradiction is a second one, related to the segregation or isolation of the educational system from daily life. Again, some segregation is necessary, for, as we have already argued, learning cannot take place without the freedom to make a mistake, and in many areas of daily life the margin for error without disastrous results is very limited. Two problems are associated with this segregation, however. The first is that when individuals, especially the young, are extracted from the main activities of the society for the purposes of learning (or, more correctly, the purposes of teaching), it becomes increasingly difficult to fit them back in. The high incidence of unemployment among young people is directly related to the fact that they have been held out of the labor market for long enough for the market to adjust to their absence. The only positions open to young people with no more than a secondary school education are those that offer low pay and little or no chance for advancement, such as packaging hamburgers at a fast-food outlet. The second problem with segregating people in school is that the skills, knowledge, and attitudes taught there increasingly are different from those demanded by employers.

There have been two responses to these circumstances, one of a traditional nature—a revival of apprenticeship—and one of more recent origin and growing popularity, programs of "cooperative education," such as those at both university and secondary school levels in which students spend as much as half of each term working full time in their area of study while continuing to be supervised by their teachers (Canada Department of Labour, 1953; Ellis, 1987). Apprenticeship programs reach into the formal school system for particular resources, but control of the programs remains outside that system. In cooperative education, the formal educational system retains control but reaches into the work world. Both types of program produce greater likelihood of employment immediately after the training period than does conventional schooling.

Immense effort and imagination have been devoted in recent years to seeking other programs that will somehow bridge the gap between the worlds of school and work (Bridging the Gap, 1988). In some countries, notably the Soviet Union, advanced educational agencies have been tied so tightly to employment, with every graduate guaranteed a job, that the gap occurs at the point of admission to those agencies rather than at graduation from them. Whether one system is preferable to the other is arguable; but the Soviet system would seem to impose limits on the development of skills other than those related to ability to complete the particular academic program.

The question becomes whether it is preferable (for the individual or the society) to be educated and possibly unemployed or to have guaranteed employment but a more limited education. On the surface, this would appear to be a conflict between the individual and the economy. Rapid and easy passage from school to work would seem to increase the efficiency of the latter and also would provide immediate employment for everyone who finished school. The price of such passage, however, is that individual choices in education would be limited to subjects and skills for which there were current economic demands. The alternative is to allow the educational system to include learning objectives besides those immediately desired by employers, with the risk that graduates would not meet employers' needs and thus would not immediately find work. When we take into account the need of the society for citizens, parents, and imaginative workers, the preferability of the latter alternative, despite all its shortcomings, becomes obvious. The choice is not a real one after all. However, if the formal educational system were redesigned and the relationship between education and learning were better understood and articulated, choosing between education and employment might not be necessary.

It is possible to incorporate the training of people of all ages into an economy in a way that benefits both the people concerned and the society as a whole (Skill Development Leave Task Force, 1983; Dupre, 1973; Thomas, Beatty, Ironside, and Herman, 1980). Many large organizations in fact do so. It means removing certain individuals temporarily from the workplace, thus providing employment from others, and preparing them for new work in more advanced positions (with the same employer or another) in the future. The value of extending the educational alternative to older people in the society lies in the fact that adults taking part in educational and learning programs have a much clearer idea than do young people of what their choices are and why they are receiving particular kinds of training.

A third contradiction within formal educational systems is the tension between their instructional and custodial functions. As educational systems have segregated more and more children and young people for longer and longer time periods, and as more and more parents of both sexes have taken jobs outside the home, both parents and employers have come to depend on the schools "babysitting" the children during these periods. The result of this dependence is that schools are asked to retain pupils for fixed lengths of time, whether this is necessary for instructional purposes or not. Yet the purpose of the school is supposed to be instruction and the methodical development of individual students, not the provision of "warehouses" for young people.

Nowhere is the conflict between educational and custodial goals felt more keenly by teacher and student alike than in the secondary school. Teachers are evaluated by others and are trained to evaluate themselves on the basis of their ability to contribute to the development of individual students. They cannot help students participate in their own growth and development, however, when both teachers and students know that the students are there only because they are forced to be, that is, when one of the functions of the educational system is to keep the students in school and out of the labor market without regard for their academic progress. This conflict, exacerbated by the fact that the students are trying to become independent adults, can become intolerable.

A fourth contradiction penetrates the very basis of public education. For the first half of the century, publicly supported schools provided the major vehicle for the socialization of children and young people. Socialization is a complex process by which, among other things, an individual comes to aspire to the sort of life that his or her society is prepared to provide and to accept societally approved means for pursuing that aspiration. At that time the schools were probably the only organizations capable of carrying out this process, integrating as they did different religious, ethnic, racial, social, and occupational groups. Today, however, radio and, especially, television appear to have taken over this integrative socializing function. Whether one approves of the content and values they convey or not, it is quite clear that broadcasting and its ancillary activities are more pervasive and powerful in the development of attitudes and expectations than are the schools.

The schools are no longer the main socializers of the young, and they are not equipped to socialize adults, either. (It has become more and more apparent that in modern societies, in which such basic elements as work, employment, family life, and sex roles are rapidly changing, socialization must be a lifelong affair.) The loss of this socializing function may not be an entirely bad thing, however. At best, it could free formal educational systems from a task that has hitherto consumed much of their energy and make it possible for them to turn their attention to other objectives that are more in tune with individual development.

Finally, systems of formal education are expensive. The costs of providing large and well-equipped physical plants, losing the productive capacity of students who are no longer children, and employing legions of teachers (whose salaries make up the major part of all educational budgets) are considerable. In the twenty years following World War II, there seemed to be no question about the value of the worldwide investment in education. Educators and others claimed that any education of any person benefited the society at least as much as, if not more than, it benefited the individual, so the cost that the society paid was justified. By the end of those two decades, however, doubt about this idea began to emerge. When older students started making demands on the formal system, the public increasingly rejected the idea that these people's education could or should be paid for in the same way as the education of the young. Citizens also began to question whether increased education really resulted in more productive employment and increased contribution to society.

All these questions resolved themselves into two major ones. First, were the formal systems of education operating as well as they could or should—that is, would improvements in their teaching methods, administrative practices, and so on bring society closer to its objectives? Second, were these formal systems the best or only means for reaching societal objectives associated with learning? In the last two decades, most governments have concluded that the answers to both questions are unknown. The only things that are clear are that the public no longer automatically accepts further expansion of educational systems and that other ways of reaching learning objectives need to be explored and supported.

Beyond Education: The Learning Environment

Formal systems of education float on a sea of learning. They have always represented only one subset of the learning objectives and learning forms present in society. Today that sea of learning is larger and more turbulent than ever before, and if we are not clear about what is taking place, it may engulf or simply wash over and bypass the formal systems as they are presently constituted. Yet, ironically, both the size and the turbulence of the learning sea results to a considerable degree from the activities of formal education over the last eighty years.

The sea of learning has increased in size in two ways. First, more people are engaging in deliberate learning over longer and longer periods of their lives. Second, these people have access to sources and types of information (far-flung computer data bases, for example) that surpass the wildest dreams of scholars of fifty years ago. The innovations in the technology of information storage and distribution that have made these changes possible have largely bypassed the educational system, however, dominated as it has been by the printed word. Talk of the "information explosion" and "information overload" often arises from people's feeling that the skills they learned in school for the selection, analysis, and judgment of information are no longer effective.

The sea has increased in turbulence partly because learning sharpens perceptions, stimulates curiosity, enlivens imagination, and releases additional energy into the pursuit of daily affairs. Turbulence has increased, too, because of the unpredictable effects of learning. Societies endure, especially politically, on the basis of assumptions about what individuals and groups know and believe and therefore what they will do. When those individuals and groups learn unexpected things — things that are not the products of a relatively predictable educational system — the assumptions no longer serve, and "all bets are off."

Specifically, educational systems have depended upon assumptions (mostly unstated) about what students will know at the time of entry into the system, what they should be taught, what they will be learning outside the system at the same time, and what they will learn after they leave the system. The explosive increase in the diversity of students' ages, backgrounds, and concurrent experience has meant that dependence on such assumptions is no longer possible. Neither, therefore, is the expectation of a uniform or predictable "character" in the system's graduates.

Illiteracy, recently acknowledged as a major problem even in so-called "developed" societies with large, established systems of formal education, provides an interesting example of the way that changes in the assumptions about prior, concurrent, and subsequent learning can affect learning outcomes. As we pointed out earlier in this chapter, with the spread of communication media that do not use print, such as the telephone, radio, and television, outside support for use of the literacy skills that children and young people learned in school began to disappear because information more and more often was exchanged by nonprint means. Much of the instruction that depended unconsciously on the presence of these supports therefore became less effective. Young people graduated from the system with both increasingly weaker literacy skills and increasing doubt about the usefulness of those skills. Bearing out that doubt, employers began to make fewer demands on literacy, causing literacy skills to decay even further.

The end result of this situation is that many young adults have become functionally illiterate or, as is sometimes said, aliterate (that is, they are able to read and write, at least to some extent, but seldom do so). This rise in functional illiteracy despite almost universal instruction in reading and writing exposes the fact that literacy skills can be extinguished if they are not used constantly. Acknowledgment of that fact has challenged and eventually changed the assumption that literacy constitutes a permanent set of skills that needs to be taught only once, during students' childhood. Formal educational systems thus discovered that they had overestimated concurrent and subsequent supports for literacy skills and at the same time had underestimated students' continuing need for access to instruction in these skills. This need is particularly acute because, as noted earlier, the increasing ubiquity of computers and accompanying devices has given the printed word a new flexibility and importance and therefore has created a new demand for literacy.

A further dramatic consequence of the growing amount of learning that takes place outside the formal educational system and its certifying power is the steady growth of the "experiential learning" or "prior learning assessment" (PLA) movement, pioneered by such agencies as the Council for Adult and Experiential Learning (CAEL) in Washington, D.C.; the Learning from Experience Trust in London; the *Fédération des cégeps* in Montreal; and similar groups in Sweden, France, and other countries. These agencies have been formed to meet growing demands for translation of activities in the Learning Domain into the marketable currency of the Education Domain, formal certificates. They allow a person to offer some measure(s) of learning accomplished outside of formal education as a basis for admission or advanced standing in certain educational programs so that the person can reenter the formal system at some point beyond that at which he or she left. This saves time and effort (and related expense) not only for the student but also for the providing agency, which does not need to repeat instruction concerning what already has been learned in another way.

While there is considerable evidence that most of the agencies promoting these procedures have taken great care to maintain their quality and integrity, individual variation in learning experiences is extreme, and the exercise of exceedingly shrewd and careful judgment in evaluating them therefore is required. Education has always had its irresponsible "diploma mills," in which cash was substituted for learning as the requirement for certification, and the PLA movement could offer the opportunity for a new form of these corrupt organizations to arise. (The form of dishonesty here is something like the dishonesty represented by the supposed buying of heavenly forgiveness, in the form of "indulgences" sold by some representatives of the Catholic Church, that so incensed Martin Luther.) The risks to society from improper certification can be reduced somewhat, however, by forging agreements between agencies, as has been done in the United States between the armed services and formal accrediting organizations (American Council for Education, n.d.). In this case programs rather than individuals are evaluated as a basis for granting "equivalent" standing.

PLA can be seen as a major contribution to the liberalizing of the certification process. It means that the acquisition of certificates can be approached from many different directions and backgrounds. It also forces reconsideration of the "residence" or involvement with special providing agencies that traditionally has been a requirement for some kinds of certification. For example, access to the examinations that result in the licensing of most professionals is contingent upon prior participation in specifically authorized instruction. On the other hand, provision of a driver's license, a certificate of considerable importance in contemporary societies, is based on an examination that does not concern itself with the way in which the examined skills were acquired. In this respect, certification achieved by means of PLA more closely resembles the awarding of driver's licenses than the granting of conventional degrees. Such certification produces a decrease in control of instruction and the means of learning.

PLA could become one successful way of bridging the gap between the formal educational system and the adult society, that is, between the Educational and the Learning domains. As we have noted, anything that bridges this gap can contribute to the continuing socialization now required by all modern societies. Even more important, it can increase the functional contact between the two domains, which strengthens the ability of the society to use both more effectively in the management of learning. On the other hand, PLA could become nothing more than a further extension of the certifying power of formal educational systems. The temptation for formal systems, everywhere faced with decline, to seek such extension will be great. Great care will be needed to protect PLA programs from dangers on both sides: loss of rigorous academic standards on one hand and lack of true respect for nontraditional learning achievements on the other.

In this chapter we have described the results of government's attempts to manage learning by deliberate direction. We have described the elements of the fundamental "form" of formal education and argued that these play a greater part in determining what is learned in the Educational Domain than does any specific content. We have also analyzed some less tangible aspects of formal education that have brought about painful contradictions in the system. Perhaps chief among these is the emphasis on preparation for life to come that sits so ill with the growing number of adult students.

Formal education, as we have seen, has distinct limits as a means of managing learning, particularly the learning of adults. Only by concentrating equally on the dynamics and opportunities of the Learning Domain and the characteristics of individual learning can we hope to meet the commitment to lifelong learning. The most important of these characteristics is that learning cannot be coerced. We can no longer try to compel people to learn, even to the extent that formal, compulsory education has done; we must find ways to persuade them to *want* to learn.

The formal educational system's commanding position in determining what will be learned, especially by adults, and how it will be learned is now being challenged. The existing system is fighting to retain that position, but under present conditions it is a lost cause. In such a struggle, learning always eventually triumphs because it is so vital and powerful a factor in individual life. The cost of the struggle, however, is likely to be measured in lost hopes, frustrated ambitions, and an impaired society. Only by more clearly understanding present conditions affecting both learning and education can we hope to recreate a vital relationship between the two.

Tension between the Education and Learning domains may be inevitable. However, if each domain is aware of what is being learned in the other and treats that learning with attention and respect, finding and using reinforcement in the other domain when possible, recognizing competition and alternative outcomes where they exist, people will be able to move more frequently and easily from one domain to the other and to benefit from the learning peculiar to each one. Such awareness also will allow societies to transfer learning objectives from one domain to the other with less conflict and disruption than occurs at present.

In the preceding chapters we have considered the learning needs engendered by particular "learning occasions" and the ways in which societies and governments have attempted to manage the learning that takes place when people try to meet these needs. In Chapter Seven we will provide a matrix or framework that can be used to analyze any group or society, past or present, in terms of its responses to the needs produced by the four types of "learning occasions." We will then conclude by making some suggestions about ways that learning management can be improved in order to maximize and take full advantage of the human capacity for lifelong learning, thus creating a true "learning society."

7

Developing
a New Perspective
on the Management
of Learning

There can be little doubt that the management of learning on an unprecedented scale is the primary concern of contemporary societies. Such societies have not been called "information societies" for nothing. The remarkable popularity of the board game *Trivial Pursuit,* with its emphasis on information that seems random or "trivial" because it exists outside a learning context, among middle classes in developed societies underlines that reality. This game was to the middle classes of the 1980s what *Monopoly,* with its emphasis on uncontrolled capitalism, was to the same classes of the Depression-dominated 1930s.

We have shown in this book that far more topics important to society involve learning than have been commonly supposed. Viewing both individual and societal changes from the perspective of learning, therefore, can produce insights that might not be gained in any other way. This "learning perspective" is likely to become increasingly useful, even vital, as we attempt to adjust to an ever more rapidly changing world. If, for example, secondary school graduates — or dropouts — could be helped to understand the distinction between the kind of learning demanded by the Educational Domain and that characteristic of the Learning Domain, the uneasy transition from one to the other made as youth shades into adulthood might becomes smoother. At the other end of the life scale, the same perspective

could help retiring citizens move from the intense, highly specialized, and nearly automatic learning associated with their employment to the more diffuse and less supported (at least at
present) learning involved in retirement. In cases like these, both
the individuals directly involved and the society as a whole need
to understand the learning dynamics central to the "learning
occasions" in question.

Looking at societal changes from a learning perspective
is perhaps even more valuable than looking at individual changes
in this way. We can gain a better understanding of many social
processes and government decisions by studying the interactions
of these things with citizens' learning. As we have seen, learning and its management influence everything from the accultu-
ration of immigrants to the effective functioning of labor unions. By studying the ways in which a society responds to its
members' learning needs and manages their learning, we can
learn much about that society's dynamics and values.

A Framework for Applying the Learning Perspective

In previous chapters we have considered the chief "learning occasions" that society must face (entry, passages, societywide
changes, and special circumstances). We also have examined
the responses to these challenges that constitute the management of learning (permitting, encouraging, directing, and forbidding). Table 1 summarizes the interaction of learning occasions and management responses in a graphic format. It provides
a framework or matrix by means of which we can analyze the
ways that groups or societies have responded to the challenges
presented by the learning needs and potentials of their members or citizens. It can help us grasp the extent of learning in
any society and understand the complex responses that individuals, groups, and governments make to learning needs.

The framework shown in Table 1 can be used to prepare
a "learning portrait" or "learning management map" for any
group or society in any historical time period. Anyone reasonably familiar with the society or organization to be studied (the
familiarity is very important) can fill in the framework with

Table 1. Managing Learning Produced by Learning Occasions.

	A. Entry	B. Passages	C. Societywide Changes	D. Exceptions
1. Permit	Constitutional rights, statutes, or bylaws	Regulatory bodies	Sunset statutes, that is, statutes with time limits	Special regulations
2. Encourage	Public support for families, voluntary organizations, commercial products, communications	Provision of resources (libraries, museums, galleries, broadcasting, parks); delegation of specific functions to private groups	Special support for voluntary organizations, special commercial products, special groups; information services; attempts at coordination	Support of voluntary organizations; provision of special services
3. Direct	Compulsory education for children; credentialing and licensing	Provision of formal education, delegation of credentialing to private groups	Increased delegation of authority to voluntary and private groups; formation of short-term administrative agencies	Special state institutions (prisons, asylums, and so on)
4. Forbid	Statutes such as abortion laws and immigration policies	Statutes such as anti-child labor laws and laws forbidding age discrimination	Statutes such as environmental protection laws; neighborhood committees to watch for compliance	Criminal law (imprisonment and so on); laws barring discrimination against handicapped

information about that society to produce the portrait. Such a portrait reveals how that society handles learning problems and meets learning needs, particularly by means other than formal education. At the same time, the "learning perspective" embodied in the matrix also helps us understand the nature and role of the formal educational system in the society in question. The nature of such systems inevitably is determined by the ways in which the society manages all of its learning problems, especially its decisions about which of those problems will be entrusted to formal education and which will remain in the Learning Domain.

Analyzing Responses to Learning Occasions

A learning management map or learning portrait can be used in a variety of ways. To begin with, it can help us examine the modes of response by which a society or human group attempts to meet the demands for learning created by a specific learning occasion. As an example, take the societywide change (C) represented by the radical changes in the roles and status of women during the past fifty years. Women have banded together in a great variety of voluntary associations to advocate and manifest this change. They have encouraged learning (both their own and that of men) related to this societywide change by creating an immense number of service and self-help groups for individual women involved in role-changing activities, such as seeking admission to previously male-dominated careers or professions (C-2). They have directed such learning by promoting and undertaking the development of women's studies in formal educational curricula and arguing for the identification and reform of male-dominant curricula (C-3). They have lobbied governments and other public and private organizations for changes in regulations and practice that would permit one kind of learning (learning to treat women fairly and equally) and forbid another (learning to discriminate against women) (C-1, C-4).

In response to the demands of women and women's groups, all levels of government in Canada, prompted initially by the courts, have made constitutional changes enhancing the legal status of women, thus permitting the learning inspired by this change (C-1). The governments have supported (both directly and indirectly) nongovernmental organizations devoted to women's issues, thereby encouraging learning (C-2). They have introduced "equal pay" laws that have corrected some of the present salary inequities between men and women in both public and private employment, and they have passed other laws that forbid the introduction or continuation of sex discrimination in employment or other contexts (C-1, C-4).

The long-term result of these actions is expected to be that women will have opportunities to learn equal to those available to men and that they will be equally able to employ the results of that learning in Canadian society. In turn, Canadian society is expected to benefit from the increased contribution of the learning of women. No modern technological society, which depends on the maximum use of all its members' intelligence and learning capacity, can afford to confine women to the limited spheres of domestic life and unskilled employment.

Categorizing responses to the learning demands resulting from various learning occasions reveals both the dynamics and the values of the society that is analyzed. If, for example, a society leaves management of one of the major learning tasks involved in "passages," the learning of the critical roles of adult life, exclusively in the hands of private interests, one is entitled to question the vitality of citizenship in that society. This can be the case when members of a nation's elite class attend private schools throughout their early years and when entry into powerful positions in business or government is restricted to members of elite organizations such as the officer corps of the armed services, certain religious orders, or families already powerful in business. Such a situation, which existed in late nineteenth and early twentieth-century Europe, resulted in more identification with class or caste than with national citizenship. This problem becomes particularly acute if the society also emphasizes highly specialized adult occupations such as law, medicine, or engineering, because the discrepancies in power and privilege are increased and the pool from which intelligent citizens can be drawn remains limited.

If, on the other hand, a society places learning tasks related to entry into adulthood under the exclusive control of large and powerful public organizations such as the political parties of socialist countries, one may doubt the vitality of individual initiative and enterprise in the society. In Eastern Europe in 1989 and 1990, for example, increasing numbers of highly trained professionals — people whose learning capacity had been stimulated systematically in the Educational Domain — found the rewards and resources available in their countries' highly organized and rigidly politicized Learning Domain increasingly unsatisfactory. They left when they could, and in their absence the existing governments eventually collapsed. When this occurred, the world witnessed the effects of these societies' failure in the management of learning.

Other examples, both of societies and of groups within them such as business corporations, can be found in abundance. We believe that our formulation allows a new insight into the way any society or group handles the individual or collective "crisis events" so common in the present world.

Comparing Different Societies

Analysis based on the framework in Table 1 also can be used to compare different societies or cultures. Ideally, a map or portrait for each society to be analyzed would be developed by natives of the society after all preparers had reached some agreement about the meaning of specific categories and terms. Comparison of the portraits would reveal that, just as learning is an intensely personal matter for each individual, the management of learning is an intensely specific series of practices for each society. Comparative studies of learning management give us a broader and more profound view of the societies in question than do traditional comparative studies of education. They also provide us with more factors in terms of which to compare the societies.

Comparisons of different societies' learning management can be especially revealing in consideration of problems related to "development," the term most often used to characterize the relationship between the rich and poor countries of the contem-

porary world. Recently the term *human resource development* has
assumed increasing prominence in discussions of development.
Use of this term reflects the fact that the rich countries have
begun to discover the futility of altering the environment of the
poorer countries by building dams, digging wells, and so on
unless they also provide systematic opportunities for the people
receiving these benefits to learn the skills and attitudes necessary for coping constructively with the changes that new technology brings.

Some critics have feared that linking *human* with *resources*
risks producing the same kind of exploitation that accompanied
the development of "natural resources" during the past century,
but we believe that such exploitation will not occur if the learning perspective is properly applied. Human resource development can mean only one thing: human beings involved in a
project learning to become something other than what they are.
They must learn skills associated with the project, whether it
is a new well for fresh water or a mill for producing steel; they
also must learn attitudes that support the skills involved and
the new way of life that use of the new technology inevitably
will bring.

They furthermore must acquire some understanding of
what their new activities will mean in terms of their own futures, the futures of their children, and the future of the community and society in which they live.

This learning cannot be exploited without the consent of
the learners because, as we have argued, one of the principal
characteristics of learning is that it cannot be coerced. Individuals must choose to learn what they learn, and this includes
choosing to learn the complex skills that are associated with most
technological projects. If the people in a society do not choose
to learn these skills, any technological project involving them
is doomed to fail. Who can forget the cry of the supervisor in
a technologically undeveloped society during World War II:
"Give us the job, and we will finish the tools!" Because the unskilled workers in the society did not know what to do with the
tools, they usually damaged them.

In short, concern with human resource development demands attention to learning, and that in turn demands attention to the way learning is managed in the society or culture in question. If certain kinds of learning, for example learning how to operate machinery or learning how to rear children, are restricted to particular groups in a society, such as people of a certain age or gender group, a new project that requires groups or individuals to learn skills or attitudes that the society has considered inappropriate will meet with little success. Such projects may appear to succeed during early stages when a good deal of general enthusiasm prevails, but in the long run the older practices and beliefs regarding what learning is appropriate for whom will prevent the proposed changes in behavior. Any educator who has worked with adults taken out of their organizations for purposes of learning new management or organizational skills knows what happens to that apparent new learning when such adults return to the social and organizational milieu from which they came and try to introduce changes prompted by the learning. The individuals may have changed, but the organization has not, and in the long run the organization is likely to prevail.

When the culture of the learners differs from that of the teacher, the problem becomes even more complex. Prospective teachers or educational planners in these circumstances first must understand that cultures differ in their beliefs about who is expected to learn what, under what circumstances, at what cost, for what reason, and with what anticipated effect. They then must discover what beliefs guide the management of learning in the culture they seek to affect. Only when these things have been done can human resource development be undertaken with any hope of success.

To begin to understand how a society manages the learning of its members, it is necessary to call on trained observers of that society, such as anthropologists, sociologists, psychologists, and, perhaps most important of all, artists. Construction of a "learning portrait" or "learning management map" within a framework like that in Table 1 also is, we would argue, a useful stage in the process of such understanding. Above all, it is important for members of Western nations, the principal sources of support for world development, to set aside their cultural bias in favor of formal education as the primary means for managing learning and try to recognize that less formal and well-articulated forms of learning management may be central to the cultures they strive to assist. Creating a learning portrait of their own society and comparing it with the portrait of the society they plan to visit can help Western observers "step out of their skins" and understand the foreign society better.

Mapping Societal Dynamics

Although the framework in Table 1 unavoidably must be presented as a static object, one of its chief uses is to reveal the dynamics associated with the management of learning. Such dynamics are the real key to understanding any society or group, for ways of managing learning are always changing. Changes in modes of learning management or responses to learning needs have become the central preoccupation of modern governments and reflect the most profound developments in a society as a whole.

We can study a society's dynamics by constructing portraits or maps of the ways it has managed its members' learning at different times in its history. By studying a series of such portraits, we can increase our understanding of how, and to some extent why, that society has developed as it has. For example, one set of learning management maps might show changes in the learning patterns involved in the training of nurses and other professionals. Until forty years ago, most nurses accomplished their needed education and learning by working under supervision, principally in hospitals. This learning thus took place largely in the Learning Domain. To a large extent this means of training provided for the learning of only a limited range of skills. It also created a certain attitude about the place of the nurse in the medical hierarchy, particularly the nurse's relationship to doctors. Since the 1960s, nurses' training has been transferred almost totally to the Educational Domain. This has resulted in new visions of nursing, new self-awareness among nurses, and new relationships with doctors. It is likely that this change also has contributed substantially to the creation of "medical teams" and new problems in the delivery of medical services. Meanwhile, the development of cooperative education in engineering, business, and to some extent medicine, in which instruction has been reduced in favor of learning on the job, presents a striking contrast to the changes in nurses' training. The results of cooperative education have yet to be examined systematically, but there is little doubt that the relationship of the professionals involved to their professional practice and to society is changing.

Another example, which we have used often in other chapters, is the steady transfer of management of learning from the Learning Domain to the Educational Domain in Western industrial societies during the past hundred years. Initially this transfer focused primarily on one group of learners (the young) and on learning needs associated with one kind of learning occasion (entry), but formal educational systems grew relentlessly and began to extend their influence and control to older groups in the society, largely through systems of credentials. Emphasis on formal education reached a peak in the late 1960s and early 1970s. Since then it has declined, for a variety of reasons, and these societies have begun to shift resources devoted to the accomplishment of learning objectives away from the Educational Domain (systems of formal education) and back to the Learning Domain. These changes have had significant effects on the societies involved, since the process and outcomes of learning tend to be quite different in the two domains. Changes in learning management occurring today are having, and will have, equally significant effects. We will discuss only a few of many possible examples.

Employee Training. One recent change in learning management in the industrial societies has been the increasing public attention and financial support given to programs of training and education provided by large and medium-sized employers, both public and private. We discussed this development in Chapter Five. As we pointed out there, the lack of clear understanding of this change is reflected by the fact that ascertaining the real extent of these programs, the numbers and types of people involved, or the total expenditures devoted to them remains almost impossible. We suspect, however, that the money spent on such programs rivals or even exceeds public expenditures on conventional education. A recent report from the United States estimates that "employers currently spend about $30 billion, 1.4 percent of the national payroll, on formal training and development. Currently, one in ten American employees gets some formal training from his or her employer" (Carnevale and Gainer, 1989, p. 48). Since these authors' inquiry did not include the armed services, the actual total spent presumably is considerably higher than the figure given.

To be sure, some of the reasons for this vacuum of information lie with the nature of the Learning Domain, of which these programs are a part. Development of effective and comprehensive accounting systems for programs in this domain, showing what people are being taught and by whom, is likely to be extremely difficult. Such programs are embedded in decentralized organizations primarily devoted to objectives other than learning, they are widely scattered within those organizations, and often they are concealed under ambiguous titles and nonspecific financial categories as well. Thus it should be no surprise that very little information is available regarding not only the size and cost of employer-sponsored programs but also the development of educational techniques and technologies, the maintenance of quality, or the protection of learners from incompetent instruction in these programs. Explicit systems for handling these things simply do not exist in the Learning Domain.

The Learning of the Elderly. As we pointed out in Chapter Four, management of the learning of elderly and retired people is also in a state of flux. This issue is growing in importance in many societies in the world, particularly the industrialized ones. One important characteristic of the elderly has been expressed in the statement that older people outgrow a society's dominant institutions; that is, they are no longer dominated by the aspirations and demands associated with career, family, and, most of all, employment. They are potentially free, therefore, to explore and learn about their world in new ways and also to arrive at new and perhaps disturbing views of that world.

Unfortunately, many societies at present seem to resent elderly people's new demand for learning and refuse to accept the legitimacy and significance of learning by older people. In particular, most Western societies feel extremely ambivalent about aging and the old, and governments in these societies so far have shown minimal appreciation of the learning potential of retired and elderly citizens. Most of what is being done in response to older people's demand for learning seems to be intended merely as pacification or busywork to keep such people "out of mischief" until they die.

Many of today's elderly have had little formal education and therefore do not make heavy demands on the Educational Domain. Instead they meet most of their learning needs through the agencies and resources of the Learning Domain, with which they are quite familiar: the family, voluntary organizations, and special-purpose public institutions such as libraries and museums. Similarly, as long as the number of nonworking older people has remained small, industrial societies have tended to leave the management of this group's learning to these agencies.

As generations pass, however, the average level of educational achievement among the elderly will increase, particularly when the "baby boomers" reach retirement age. The demand of this group upon the Educational Domain is likely to increase concomitantly. Such demand probably will be presented, at least initially, through traditional vehicles of the Learning Domain such as membership organizations. The demands currently made by the few educated elderly are likely to be forerunners of what is to come.

Two of these membership organizations present interestingly contrasting approaches to meeting the learning and educational needs of the elderly. One group, Elderhostel, is an independent organization created largely by educational agencies. It organizes short-term educational opportunities, entirely noncredit, for thousands of retired people throughout the developed world. "Third Age" organizations, by contrast, are controlled by the retired and elderly themselves. They negotiate with educational agencies to arrange educational programs for their members. The distinction between the two approaches is likely to be significant in terms of the independence of older people as learners and as citizens.

China has responded to the learning demands of its older population by creating "universities" for them. Such an action suggests either considerable confidence in the agencies of the Educational Domain or, perhaps, a wish to maintain control over people who are no longer under the domination of major institutions in order to forestall possible political mischief wrought by "idle hands." Indeed, the problems and opportunities inherent in managing the learning of retired people are likely to receive greater attention throughout the world as the number of such people grow, simply because one institution that the elderly do not outgrow is politics. They remain citizens and voters until death, and increasingly they will be able to back up their learning demands with political clout.

Regardless of how the learning needs of the elderly are met, attempting to accommodate these new learning demands may produce social problems. Emphasis on the agencies of the Learning Domain potentially offers the warmth of membership and the satisfactions of social action, but it may also encourage some of the more destructive phenomena of "age politics." Organizations based on age, like other special interest groups, often seek political advantages for themselves at the expense of others in the society. The greater time that retired people have at their disposal sometimes allows the groups they form to have a greater influence than their numbers warrant, and other groups often resent this influence, since the elderly's extra free time is often perceived to be purchased by public support in the form of government-sponsored retirement benefits. Politics based on age can be as destructive as politics based on race, because neither age nor race can be changed by learning.

On the other hand, emphasis on the Educational Domain, with its expense and focus on the relatively isolated student role, could result in greater isolation of the elderly from the rest of society. Experience with educational programs for the elderly in Japan has generated some concern about lack of opportunities for them to use their new learning, for example.

Obviously we will have to try to achieve some balance in utilization of the two domains and also between acknowledging and nourishing the capacity and will of the elderly to learn as they choose and making the combined outcomes of their lengthy experience and their new learning available throughout the society. This can be done only if we examine the lives of the elderly from a learning perspective. Persuading societies to do this will be a considerable achievement.

Learning Related to Health. A final area of change in learning, one that has so far received little attention from this perspective, is health. The most dramatic changes in this area, which provide a classic case study in the dynamics of learning management, concern the AIDS epidemic that is currently sweeping the world. The learning perspective allows us to analyze responses to this terrible disease in a new and useful way.

When AIDS first appeared, everyone assumed that it was a problem related to only one group in society, homosexuals. It therefore was treated as an example of "exceptions." As such it garnered only modest amounts of public and private funds, which supported a limited variety of therapeutic and educational programs and voluntary organizations. Once people became aware that the disease could affect the general population, however, it began to be treated as a societywide change. All three domains then were called upon to deal with the learning problems that the epidemic presented.

So far, none of them has met this challenge very well. Membership (voluntary) groups can respond quickly and personally to what are perceived to be limited problems, and with sufficient resources they can be very effective and efficient. However, in order to obtain sufficient resources they must engage in public advocacy, which necessarily involves the society as a whole. Eventually *ad hoc,* "crisis" learning will be transferred to learning mediated by the formal educational system, which tends to depersonalize and institutionalize responses to the situation.

Concern for the prevention of the spread of AIDS carries with it attitudes toward sex and health that will be generalized beyond this specific issue and will be associated with public authority, as are all other attitudes incorporated into the educational system.

In the past, private voluntary groups in Western societies usually dissolved once they were able to attract the public attention and support that led to creation of government-financed programs that supported their causes. These groups seem to have discovered the limits of the state's ability to manage learning in recent years, however, so such dissolution no longer happens automatically. Thus it probably is not surprising that the education campaign to stop the spread of AIDS, involving as it does the two most intimate and personal of all human aspirations, learning and loving, in most countries has remained in private hands.

Other aspects of the provision of health services also can be viewed from a learning perspective. For example, many chronic diseases are not curable but can be controlled to some extent by the afflicted individuals. The classic example of such an illness is diabetes, which is now occurring at an alarming rate among middle-aged adults in Western societies. Because this disease is managed through diet and insulin injections, diabetics must learn new information about what to eat and in some cases must learn the skill of injecting the hormone at appropriate times. In a sense, diabetics must become their own doctors.

Many forms of cancer and heart ailments, like diabetes, have come to be seen as diseases that people can learn to manage. As a result, a substantial enterprise has developed within health services to meet these new learning needs. Except for the training in new attitudes toward health care that is beginning to appear in medical school curricula, this learning has been entrusted entirely to the Learning Domain, where it is administered through such agencies as volunteer organizations and hospitals. Eventually, however, most of the learning may be transferred to the Educational Domain.

The importance of learning's role in the treatment of

chronic illness will continue to grow as more people live longer and thus become subject to these kinds of disease and also as doctors learn more about the prevention and management of illness. This new stress on learning means that sick people must learn skills formerly confined to health care specialists, such as nutritional management or use of hypodermic needles. At the same time, health care workers must learn the skills needed to transform themselves from authoritarian sources of direct treatment and instructions into teachers and facilitators of learning. "Treatment of a patient" must become "negotiation with a client."

In this chapter we have tried to demonstrate how the "learning perspective" and a matrix that shows the interaction of learning occasions and learning management responses can be used to analyze groups, organizations, and entire societies. This perspective can be used to analyze the effects of particular learning moments, compare different groups, study the changes in learning management that occur in single groups over time, and increase understanding of what is taking place in a group or society at a particular point in history. Today, when intelligence and imagination are becoming much more important than muscle and physical endurance as tools for dealing with an increasingly complex world, the human capacity for learning must take center stage. The perspective of learning therefore becomes a, if not the, principal one needed to understand and nurture human society.

The final chapter in this book will make some suggestions about ways that learning management can be improved in order to maximize and take full advantage of the human capacity for lifelong learning. We will first consider the implications of some of the characteristics of learning discussed earlier. We will then discuss ways to expand learning resources, to change the educational system in order to involve more feedback from the Learning Domain and emphasize lifelong "continuing education," and finally, to create a true "learning society."

8

Creating a Society
of Lifelong Learners

The modern world demands that people learn all through their lives, and increasing numbers of adults, in turn, are demanding access to learning and educational resources. As a result of these twin demands, modern statecraft is becoming little more than the proper management of learning. No matter where on the scale of economic, social, and political development a society finds itself or what type of government it has, that government has little choice but to acquire the skills required to manage learning. These skills include a clear understanding of the functions of the various domains and of the consequences of support or lack of it for any of them. The tendency of modern totalitarian states has been to limit the activities of the Social Domain, suppress or try to co-opt those of the Learning Domain, and maximize those of the Educational Domain. Such a policy appears bound to fail. The maximization of human learning capacity, on the other hand, engenders a new relationship between the individual and the state that we are only beginning to understand. It is clear, however, that this relationship must be based on freedom to learn and to choose learning objectives.

This book has charted the rise and fall of the belief that direction of learning by means of the formal educational system (what we have called the Educational Domain) was the only or even the best means of managing learning. The tendency of governments, especially those in Western industrialized societies, to translate virtually all learning needs into educational needs has declined considerably since its midcentury peak. Today the presence of severe economic and social problems that education has not solved, the increasing number of adults with strongly expressed learning needs that the educational system could not meet, the rising cost of formal education, technological changes in the way people store, transfer, and use information, and a number of other factors have shown clearly the limits of formal education and have brought a resurgence of interest in and support for learning in the Learning Domain.

Behavior characteristic of the Learning Domain, which for the past century has been regarded as essentially private, now is becoming a matter of considerable public concern. It therefore is extremely important that we understand the nature of that behavior. One reason for this importance is that learning, especially in the Learning Domain, can be the cause of significant social conflict. The first kind of conflict is most common in the early stages of mobilization, when demands on learning are being extended over populations and lifetimes for the first time. At this point there may be severe conflict between two ways of life, one committed to constant individual change and the other to maintaining traditional, predictable ways. Such conflict arises not only in whole societies but also in many smaller groups and organizations within any society.

The second danger, a more common and persistent one, arises when substantial groups of people in a single society are pursuing sharply different, even mutually exclusive learning objectives. For example, we have already referred to the fact that in industrial societies over the past forty years, the one-third to one-half of the adult population that takes part in formal educational programs is composed overwhelmingly of those who have already succeeded in the initial stages of their education (Johnstone and Rivera, 1965; Devereaux, 1985). We have noted that it would be a serious mistake to assume that those who do not participate in such formal programs are not learners. They are simply pursuing learning objectives other than those provided for by the agencies of formal education. These people live almost entirely in the Social and Learning domains, with little or no contact, except as children, with the Educational Domain. We strongly suspect that the present literacy programs in these societies, concentrating as they do on the mechanisms of the Learning Domain, are as much intended to bring these dispersed learners into the activities, objectives, and values of the Educational Domain as they are to teach the skills of literacy. This reflects a growing understanding that no society can survive highly polarized differences in the learning objectives of its citizens.

If the pursuit of opposing learning objectives involves substantial numbers of a nation's citizens and persists over a long time, that nation may find itself in serious danger of collapse. The conflict between the French- and English-speaking populations of Canada offers a striking example of such a threat. The fact that the French-speaking minority has exclusive control of a "sovereign" province, Quebec, means that the existence of competing learning objectives is fortified by possession of the instruments of a state. Quebec, as the "French State" within Canada, wishes more political and economic control for the protection of that "Frenchness" than most existing federations will permit to one of their constituents — at least so far. Many English-speaking Canadians, in turn, resent the need to learn to speak French in order to participate in their national government. Because nationhood has tended to be identified with having a single ethnic and, even more important, linguistic identity, which implies very specific learning objectives, the conflict between the objectives of these two different ethnic and linguistic groups has offered a serious threat to the continuation of the Canadian national state. Similar situations can be found in, for example, Lebanon and the Soviet Union.

One reason that knowledge of what members of a particular population are learning is essential to a modern government, then, is that it can detect potentially conflicting learning objectives and offer an opportunity to search for compromise and other objectives that can be shared. Other reasons are more positive. If feedback between the Learning and the Educational domains is established, the former can penetrate, enliven, and reform the latter so that both can play the most active and effective parts possible in meeting citizens' learning needs. The learning needs of citizens today and, even more, in the future are so great that society needs to do everything possible to maximize their capacity to meet those needs.

Understanding the Learning Domain

A recent report of results from a poll taken among a random sample of the Canadian adult population showed most respondents to be seriously ignorant or misinformed about a wide range of scientific phenomena, with the partial exception of those related to health and the environment ("Read It and Weep . . . , 1990). The predictable official comment was that these people must have been badly taught in school, and it was followed by the usual call for improved science instruction.

Another interpretation is possible, however. It is important to note that the areas in which people seemed better informed are presently prominent on the public agenda and therefore in the daily press. We suspect that little of what people knew about these subjects had been learned in school. Rather, it had been acquired through the media, as a result of both personal and public concern. In seeking to correct the defects that surveys of this kind show, it may be more important to concentrate on how, where, and why people learned what they do know rather than on what and why they do not know. Once we discover which sources of learning were effective—and they are unlikely to have been those of formal education—we can perhaps harness them to make up what society sees as learning deficits.

Because learning has such an influence on behavior, a modern government must be constantly and acutely aware of what its citizens are learning and what learning objectives they are pursuing. Information on these points, we believe, is much more important to gather than information on what citizens either know (as evidenced by public opinion polls) or are being taught (as evidenced by data from education providing agencies), which are the main kinds of learning-related information that governments collect at present. Such information misses the essential dynamics of the society. To know what people are learning, on the other hand, is to know where their hopes and aspirations are, what they care about, where their hearts and minds are, what they believe their society is about. To know what a society's people are learning is to understand that society more profoundly than ever has been possible before.

The key questions that any contemporary government must answer are who is (and who ought to be) learning what, under what circumstances, at whose expense, to what end, and with what success. Satisfactory or unsatisfactory answers to those questions are likely to determine the success or failure of the government. We suggest that a "learning index," based on regular surveys of what people are learning, how, why, and at what cost, is as important to a contemporary society's understanding of itself as is the Gross National Product, the Consumer Price Index, or figures on the incidence of unemployment. In addition to its value to governments, this information can be extremely valuable to a country's citizens because it can tell them, more accurately than anything now available, what their fellow citizens really care about.

Techniques for the regular collection of information about what people are learning, as distinct from what they know or what they have been taught, are already available (Tough, 1979; Thomas, MacKeracher, MacNeil, and Selman, 1982). Basically, they are the techniques used in making public surveys. Because this information is vital to individuals as well as governments, it should never be the private possession of the state. Rather, it should be collected, supervised, and regularly reported by an independent public body. The information, furthermore, should be collected in a way that respects the privacy and autonomy of individual learners. If this is not done, people will misrepresent their learning endeavors or refuse to report them at all.

Recognizing Implications of
Learning Domain Characteristics

In order to understand better how to take advantage of the Learning Domain, we need to consider the implications of some of the characteristics of that domain that we described in Chapter Three. First, as we pointed out in that chapter, the Learning Domain is a place of intense activity. It is the heart of the contemporary mobilized society. Individuals within it play active rather than passive roles. The principal mode of government response to this domain is encouragement, as opposed to the permission or forbidding offered to the Social Domain and the direction characteristic of the Educational Domain.

Because the Learning Domain is so active, governments need to be aware of the activities in this domain all the time. They cannot afford to wait until the next election, when the outcomes of those activities will express themselves formally. Many democratic governments have responded to the growing power of the Learning Domain by trying to monitor it through public opinion polls, but these polls, as we have noted, usually ask the wrong questions. Some totalitarian governments, on the other hand, have come to understand, albeit dimly, that power can be maintained by manipulating or co-opting elements of the Learning Domain. This is the true meaning of Ellul's (1967) comment that the life of a citizen in a contemporary totalitarian state is one of perpetual enthusiasm. Such manipulation cannot succeed for long, however, particularly if the population involved has gained experience with managing its own learning.

Second, the evidence of the Learning Domain, as we have described it, in itself reflects how widespread learning is in modern societies. Those who view learning as a relatively rare phenomenon have been misled by the general preoccupation with formal education. The only thing that has been in short supply has been the will or ability to learn what the educational system has to teach.

Third, learning is frequently unconscious, submerged in the pursuit of some other objective or objectives. Investigations in this area (Tough, 1979; Fair, 1973; Denys, 1973) reflect the care that must be taken to discover what individuals actually have been or are learning, since most people are likely to recognize and acknowledge only the kind of learning that they associate with formal education; that is, with being taught something. Many people in fact demonstrate learning skills of considerable sophistication without being aware of them.

Finally, the Learning Domain is characterized by optimism and good nature. People are at their best when they are learning. They are alert, enthusiastic, and receptive to and supportive of learning in others, and they are usually quite delighted when their own learning is recognized (Thomas, MacKeracher, MacNeil, and Selman, 1982).

The support of learning offered by other learners is particularly valuable because learning can be a source of fear and uncertainty to those not involved in the process. This fear is caused by the fact that the outcomes of a learning project cannot be predicted by either learners or their associates. Fear of unexpected outcomes of learning may explain our public preference for learning that results only from teaching, which offers the illusion of a predictable, safe outcome. Learning can make us seem like strangers to those closest to us — indeed, even to ourselves — and strangers, as history and literature tell us, are constantly in danger because they are perceived as threats, that is, stimuli to learning with unpredictable outcomes.

These characteristics of learning make it extremely difficult to guess the effects of the societal mobilization resulting from increased emphasis on the capacity of citizens to learn. The only thing we can be sure of is that this change will produce a profound alteration in the relationship between individuals and the state and between individuals and any group to which they belong.

As Chapter One explained, other characteristics of learning are that learning cannot be coerced, is irreversible, involves duration, and is influenced by other human beings. Although these characteristics are inextricably interrelated, we will review them separately.

Learning Cannot Be Coerced. No one can be compelled to learn anything. Relatedly, no two people will learn exactly the same thing even when exposed to the same learning stimulus. Each person will put his or her own stamp on the material to be learned, investing in the process and outcome all that he or she has already learned: that is, an entire self. Even in the most inflexible educational situation, the learner can make the individual contribution of learning to despise the subject matter, hate the teacher, or both.

In our increasingly technological society, learning objectives must include not only knowing how to perform a technical operation but desiring to perform it as well as possible. Achievement of this latter objective obviously is possible only with the willing involvement of the learner. The Educational Domain offers the illusion of control over learners' behavior through various punishments and rewards. In the Learning Domain, however, no such control even appears possible. As the maintenance and development of modern states come to depend more and more on the learning of all citizens, the use of force as a means of control is likely to become even less successful than it has been in the past.

Instead of using force, which reduces and limits people's learning activity, governments need to encourage learning through persuasion, which involves constant activity. Persuasion is the mainspring of mobilization. It requires seeing citizens as active rather than passive, in contrast to past visions of the "masses." In a society based on persuasion rather than coercion, the individual must be free to consider the alternatives proposed and to withdraw attention and participation from any of them.

In the mobilized society, the society harnessed to continuous change or development, the relationship between the citizen and the state must be dynamic and constantly renewed. To be sure, it will remain open to abuse and corruption, just like the relationship between citizen and state in the past. Indeed, a society based on the mobilization of learning capacity presents more rather than less moral ambiguity than previous societies, precisely because the outcomes of learning cannot be predicted or controlled either by the individuals concerned or by the state. For example, the government of Canada undertook a program of energy conservation in the mid-1970s with the intent of reducing the amount of money spent on oil and other fuels. Citizens learned how to reduce their energy use so effectively that they upset the plans of the large public and private fuel suppliers, with the result that their change in behavior was ignored when supplies of conventional fuel became more available. In the late

1980s the need for fuel conservation reappeared, this time spurred by environmental rather than financial considerations, and new programs of public education were produced. It is too soon to tell how the Canadian public will respond this time, but it seems likely, unfortunately, that the last campaign "taught" them to distrust the motives of those who preach energy conservation. They therefore may offer only limited cooperation with conservation efforts.

Although learning offers no guarantee that a government will not attempt to manipulate its citizenry, learning does provide some safeguards precisely because it cannot be coerced. Because the modern state must depend on the learning capacity of its citizens, it is obliged to acknowledge, if not accept, the outcomes of their learning. This leads to increased autonomy and self-determination for citizens and perhaps even to establishment of the sort of relationship between the state and the individual that the founders of democratic states envisioned.

The classical skills needed for citizenship in a democratic society — consultation, discussion, and evaluation of public enterprise — could be raised to new heights in a learning-centered society. The increased influence and activity of private voluntary groups, such as those active in environmental, health, and feminist affairs, are reflections of the possible new politics of learning. Such groups may seem like irritating aberrations, especially to those whose plans they oppose, but in fact they are a proper elaboration of democratic procedures and the inescapable result of a society's increased dependence on learning.

Learning Is Irreversible. The discovery of the means to release atomic power, the "sorcerer's apprentice" of the modern world, is the outstanding example of the fact that learning is irreversible. Once we had learned to manipulate the forces of the atom, we could never return to the innocence of a world that lacked that knowledge. The possession of a technical capacity that for moral reasons cannot be exercised, formerly a problem restricted to individuals (the medical doctor's ability to kill a patient, for example, or the accountant's ability to embezzle funds without detection), now has become a phenome-

non of global importance. Training, agreed-on codes of behavior, and the influence of powerful peers restrain most individuals from criminal use of their special skills, but, until recently, large groups and nations have felt no similar requirement
to hold back. This century's two world wars provide the most
terrible example of the technocratic fallacy that if you are able
to do something, you are not only entitled but obliged to do
it. Uneasy restraint has emerged, however, in respect to use
of atomic weapons, and it may be developing for technologies
that threaten the environment as well.

A new morality based on learning is slowly but steadily
beginning to influence all of private and public life. This moral
imperative states that all learning must result in the enhancement
of further learning, both for ourselves and for others. Immorality, therefore, results when learning outcomes impede further
learning. The use of atomic weapons represents that negative
potential on the largest scale of all, since killing obviously ends
the learning of those killed. Immorality can be defined in this
way on a smaller scale as well, however. The learning of criminal skills, for example, potentially results in reduced further
learning for the criminal because of the restrictions of imprison-
ment. Perhaps more important, it also results in the destruction of the confidence of the criminal's victims in their ability
to learn how to protect themselves and their property. The irreversibility of learning means simply that all learning must contribute to its own furtherance. The individual who truly learns
something is both motivated and obliged to share that learning
with others, specifically by assisting them to learn it themselves.
There must be no limits to learning except those imposed by
finite lives.

Learning Takes Time. The third important characteristic of learning is that it involves duration. No matter how urgent the need or how great the determination, the requirement
of time for learning cannot be evaded: pipers must have time
to learn their tunes, no matter who the payer is or how large
the payment. People may not allow themselves time enough for
learning, or they may be deceived (or deceive themselves) that

they have learned something quickly when in fact they have not. Thomas Hobbes, no great admirer of humankind, observed in *Leviathan* that nothing seduces a man quite so much as to be told that he is a facile learner.

The fact that learning requires time also means that governments must allow time for citizens to learn whatever must be learned in order to effect major social changes. Because learning cannot be coerced, citizens must also learn *why* they are expected to learn certain things. Even generals know that their troops need to understand something about the broader dimensions of the battle in which they are engaged (Williams, 1983). That learning also takes time.

An example of the need to allow time for learning can be found in the regulatory hearings to which major construction projects or other developments are subjected in most industrial countries today before they can proceed. These hearings solicit opinions about the impact of a project from a variety of public and private sources, including those that represent unpopular or minority views. Canada has developed a practice of providing public support for groups that otherwise would be unable to appear before regulatory bodies to express their opinions. This practice echoes the words of former Canadian Chief Justice Thomas Berger, who, during his investigation of the effects of economic development on the MacKenzie River Valley, is reputed to have said to one group wishing to appear that the group might not represent the public interest, but it was in the public interest that they be heard (Berger, 1976).

Solicitation and presentation of all these diverse opinions can make hearings of this kind seem endless, particularly to those who want to get on with the proposed project. The learning involved, however, contributes not only to the improvement of the project but to the enhanced quality of individual and collective life. As a result of these public exchanges, the executors of the projects learn about possible unanticipated consequences of their actions, the groups contributing to the hearing learn how their opinions relate to those of other groups and gain practice in the skills of preparing information and presenting it publicly, and the public learns about the true dimensions and implications of the project in question and of others like it. To be sure, it takes skill to manage such hearings — skill in judging who ought to be heard, skill in listening, skill in knowing when to conclude the exchanges. Good intentions without these skills can, and frequently do, persuade citizens that such exchanges are a sham, that no one is really listening to the opinions offered, and that nothing of consequence or truth can be learned from the proceedings.

Not all events are or seem to be amenable to the processes of public consultation, that is, to the provision of opportunities for people to learn to cope with them. But even when providing time for learning really does seem impossible, as with natural disasters, the problems are likely to repeat themselves until opportunities for such learning are found or made. That is what prevention really means. On other occasions the lack of time for learning is more apparent than real, resulting merely from manipulation of the public in the interest of some private will. In these cases the public is demeaned and the will to learn is reduced. Sooner or later, time for learning must be allowed.

Learning Depends on Other People. The last major characteristic of learning we wish to review is its dependence on the influence of other people. As we have noted, it is this dependence that makes freedom of association even more important than the other basic freedoms. Without freedom of association, freedom of speech seems an empty right. With freedom of association, some freedom of speech is assured.

Each person, by virtue of his or her learning, is unique. He or she is also an irreplaceable potential source of learning for others. These beliefs, even if they are not consciously reflected upon, lie behind the use of collective bodies such as boards, committees, juries, and cabinets, a practice well established in the political life of democratic societies. Even military regimes involve juntas and councils, though they usually operate in the interests of a single individual. The use of such bodies demonstrates the value of applying the enhanced learning of a small group of people to the conduct of public affairs.

To be sure, popular wisdom exhibits ambivalent feelings

about collective action, as shown in the contradictory aphorisms "Many hands make light work" and "Too many cooks spoil the broth." This ambivalence may reflect feelings about responsibility. Societies have been reluctant to assign collective responsibility, and the belief that each individual must accept and act upon responsibility for his or her own learning and resulting behavior is fairly and properly embedded in most legal codes. Thus there is an unavoidable tension between the functional value of collective management and the necessity for individual responsibility. It is a productive tension, however: trying to maximize the advantages of both approaches is worth the risks of overdependence on either. In the West we have focused on developing the skills of individual responsibility and only recently have begun to pay serious attention to skills of collective management. By contrast, certain other cultures, such as that of Japan, have emphasized and become very skilled in the collective approach. Both approaches require skill to maintain, and both are valuable to individuals and to society.

Technological developments in communication are rapidly altering the ways in which people associate with each other. Printed matter (books, magazines, newspapers) and the postal system, which depended on and encouraged conventional literacy, were the foundations of communication in the modern state. In recent decades, however, the telephone, radio and television broadcasting, and especially the computer, linked to the electronic ganglia of the previous two media, have caused profound alterations in our means of communicating (associating over distance) and the learning that results from that association.

The telephone allowed some of the qualities of oral exchange, originally the communication medium of small groups in direct contact with each other, to be extended over larger spaces. Today the computer provides a means of instant distribution of the printed word over distance that is comparable to what the telephone provides for speech. Furthermore, unlike the broadcasting technologies that have dominated the past fifty years, the telephone and the computer allow people to make interactive responses like those of personal communication. Both thus allow people at a great distance from each other to associate in ways that formerly were possible only for people who could be in face-to-face contact.

These new communications media have been distributed very unevenly among citizens, however. Radio and television spread very rapidly through huge populations, but access to the more individually responsive devices, especially computers, has been limited to the relatively wealthy and powerful. These changes in communication therefore have contributed to the uneven distribution of learning opportunities and objectives rather than ameliorating them.

Maximization of learning potential means maximization of chances for association. If nations with large land masses and widely separated populations (such as Australia, Canada, the United States, and the Soviet Union) wish to survive, they will have to intervene in the present patterns of dissemination and use of communication devices. It is urgent to find the electronic equivalent of the low postal rates that made communication between small organizations and widely spread members of larger ones possible in the past. Community centers that provide public access to computers and related communication devices, copiers, facsimile transmitters, equipment for small-scale radio and television production, and the like are going to become as necessary to the support of democratic society as post offices, public libraries, and telephone exchanges have been in the past. Recent experiments with mobile community television transmission (Department of University Extension and Continuing Studies, 1987), in which members of communities were encouraged to see themselves on television and produce their own television programs, provide an example of promising developments. Provision of such opportunities on a much larger scale will be required, however, if the world's large nation-states are to survive. If the learning among small groups of people within a society becomes exclusive, that society cannot endure.

Expanding Learning Resources

Maximization of activities in the Learning Domain requires direct intervention by the state in the form of creation and maintenance of such learning resource agencies as libraries, art galleries, museums, and parks. These agencies are the "balance wheels" of the Learning Domain. They reflect the values of the society in that they offer help in achieving the learning objectives that the society deems most desirable. Their importance is incalculable because they are intended for citizens to use through free choice.

We know much less about these agencies than we should. We are informed regularly of the extent of expenditures on education, but only rarely (with the possible exception of the regular contention over the conditions of public broadcasting) do the costs and use of these "cultural agencies" receive public attention. Yet public expenditure on the Learning Domain and its agencies ought to be, and probably is (if we include expenditures by industry and the armed services), greater than the amount spent on the Educational Domain by a considerable margin. Information about the agencies of the Learning Domain should be included in the "learning index" that we have proposed.

We also need to be more imaginative about extending the range of public learning agencies. Computer software, videotapes, and the like must be made available through agencies resembling public libraries, or through libraries themselves, as soon as possible. We cannot afford to leave their distribution to the vagaries of the market for as long as books were left before the introduction of public libraries. Making these learning resources available to everyone regardless of wealth or education will show citizens that our society regards such resources as legitimate and intensely stimulating sources of learning. Not effecting this distribution, on the other hand, will result in increasing division among learners and thus greater divisions within society.

The widespread availability of popular music through radio broadcasting and public libraries in the industrial societies created a new politics in that it produced a new awareness and sense of identity in its audience. As a result of this new sense of identity, the popular music audience developed an ability to respond to events as a unified worldwide group, as was demonstrated in their reaction to the Live-Aid concert. The same kind of effect may result from public distribution of videotapes and computer hardware and software. If the politics is to be valid, we must be sure that users of these new learning resources are drawn from as wide a spectrum of the population as possible.

Maximization of the Learning Domain's value and use also requires governments to delegate responsibility for achievement of certain learning objectives to agencies outside the formal educational system. This means withdrawing some forms of certification from the educational system's control. To a degree this has already happened in certain highly regulated industries, such as aviation, and we can learn a great deal from the experience of those industries. The transfer to unfamiliar settings of skills and practices formerly limited to agencies of formal education can be and is being done, but it takes time and will require much real learning on the part of everyone involved. It is particularly important to keep these changes as expansions of the Learning Domain and resist the temptation to expand the Educational Domain to cover them instead.

Changing the Educational Domain

Much of the current literature on adult education (Knowles, 1984; Brundage and MacKeracher, 1980) maintains a certain mythology about adult learning. Although this material claims to discuss adult learning, what most of it actually presents is information on how adults may best be taught what an education providing agency wants to teach them (Long, 1983). There is nothing wrong with teaching agencies improving their ability to deal with adult students; after all, those students have entered the agencies voluntarily in order to obtain what the agencies provide. What is dangerous is to confuse the procedures of teaching agencies and their students with the procedures of the Learning Domain and its learners. Only by becoming more cognizant of both the Learning and the Educational domains and the differences between them can practitioners of adult education avoid this pitfall.

The growing prominence of the Learning Domain necessitates changes in the Educational Domain. It is clear that we can no longer expect the latter to help us meet all or even most of our learning needs. Instead, resources for learning will have to be shared on a larger scale than ever before. The Educational Domain needs to respond to the growth of the Learning Domain, not by either ignoring or trying to capture the learning of the latter but rather by acknowledging, respecting, and complementing its activities and processes. The formal system of education will need to adjust its programs to recognize what can be learned more effectively in the Learning Domain, accepting that some valuable learning objectives cannot be achieved through education or teaching. These adjustments probably will affect older, voluntary students the most, but they will have some application to younger, compulsory students as well.

One possible useful change in the relationship of the two domains would be an extension of the idea of cooperative education, now applied mostly at the higher levels of instruction, to many more subjects and to more kinds of education. The basic principle of cooperative education is having students learn outside of a school setting, supervised partly by teachers or employers. The learner-student and the teacher or employer must cooperate to make the experience meaningful.

Obtaining Feedback from the Learning Domain. It would be difficult to overemphasize the importance of education providing agencies maintaining as much contact as they can with learners (as opposed to students) — that is, with people who are not interested in formal programs or certification but rather are trying to solve problems that they have defined for themselves. Such contact provides direct and continuous experience in the translation of learning needs into educational needs.

Different countries have worked out different means by which educational agencies can share their resources with independent adult learners. These include the formation of special educational agencies, for example the Scandinavian Folk Universities, and the provision of noncredit academic work in regular educational agencies in North America, Britain, Australia, and other countries. Unfortunately, all such programs presently are regarded as marginal by the main educational systems of the countries in question. They are rarely appreciated for what they can be, that is, an invaluable source of information about the Learning Domain and therefore a basis for the effective adjustment of the educational agency. Intellectually and academically, programs of this kind truly are and indeed must be marginal, in that they deal with unconventional groups and individuals in society and treat unconventional formulations of knowledge in unfamiliar ways. That marginality, however, must not be confused with marginality in importance to the parent agency. To cripple such programs is to cripple the flexibility of the entire agency and the educational system of which it is a part.

Faculty members in postsecondary educational institutions traditionally have designed their own programs with little feedback from outside, thus maintaining the educational system's isolation. By contrast, technical colleges in recent years have developed extensive systems of advisory committees composed of practitioners, and professional schools in universities have a long tradition of consultation with their professional bodies. The development, halting and uneven as it is, of in-service training for teachers at all levels of the existing system provides a new and presently underused mechanism for the continuous review of educational programs by those "on the firing line." However, such endeavors will need far more time and attention from both administrators and faculty members if they are to become flexible and complete enough to be effective in providing feedback from the Learning Domain.

The increasing presence of adult students at all levels of education provides a new and indispensable source of information on which to base the continuous adjustment of teaching programs. These students inevitably bring with them intense and relatively conscious current experience of the Learning Domain. If the validity of their experience is recognized and systematized by means of constant, regular, planned consultation with instructors, teaching agencies can gain an invaluable resource. Unfortunately, few teaching agencies so far seem to have taken advantage of this resource or even shown any interest in trying. Learners who enter the educational system become students, and students, except perhaps the most advanced ones, usually are considered only as objects of teaching rather than as possible subjects of learning.

As we have noted, all educational systems operate on assumptions about what their students have learned before they enrolled, what they are learning both inside and outside of class during their student period, and what they will learn after the completion of their studies. We believe that most of the difficulties presently encountered by formal systems of education arise from the fact that these assumptions are no longer accurate. A system devoted to collecting information about what people in a society are learning (as distinct from what they are taught), as we suggested earlier, would provide not only recognition of the significance of the Learning Domain but also essential information that would help educational institutions update their assumptions and thus provide more effective teaching.

Establishing a System of Continuing Education. The most fitting response of formal education to the new prominence of the Learning Domain would be the establishment of a system of true "continuing education" (Thomas and others, 1981). We use this term to mean not merely formal education undertaken after initial formal schooling has been completed, as the popular usage has it, but what the term really implies: a system that offers educational opportunity from the most elementary stage to the farthest reaches of advanced study; that includes students who are compelled to attend and those who choose to; that is accessible to persons of any age, at any level suitable to their academic abilities; that is made up of a variety of providing agencies; and that provides programs of both a credit and a noncredit character. Most of the world's formal educational systems are moving in this direction, but the overall concept of continuing education as defined here has been slow to emerge.

Above all, a formal system that emphasizes continuing education as we define it will be concerned with learning itself; that is, with helping students learn how to learn. Elementary education in such a system will be devoted principally to helping students become fluent in what might be called the languages of learning. Three of these "languages" are the familiar "reading, writing, and 'rithmetic." There are, however, many other languages of learning that are less well recognized (especially in current educational programs) but equally valid, including speech, graphic art, music, physical movement (expressed through athletics and dance), and personal exchange. Even when these are taught, they tend to be regarded as marginal frills for student dilettantes or a few specially talented "geniuses."

In a world dominated, as the contemporary world is, by radio, television, and film, it is almost impossible to understand the indifference of existing educational systems to the importance of the languages of these communications media. This indifference has cost the schools in industrial societies their central place in socialization of the young. Although we suggested earlier that there were some advantages in allowing the schools to surrender the task of socialization to the mass media, it may be desirable after all for the educational system to regain control of at least part of that task. Contemporary society is so complex and volatile that more than one source of socialization seems essential.

Recovery of the educational system's role in socialization should be possible in the context of genuine continuing education, which would affect both the socialization of the young and the repeated socialization of adults. In order to play a significant part in socializations, schools will have to accept responsibility for deliberately aiding their students to develop the skills needed for learning effectively in the Learning Domain. Such skills include the skills of working in groups, identifying relevant learning resources, and, most important of all, being able to evaluate one's own learning achievement.

Systems of formal education turn learners into students. Plenty of people in the world, particularly adults, apparently wish to make this change. Educational systems need to be reconfigured in a way that will help these people enter the student world as simply and smoothly as possible. One reason that learning often is a frightening enterprise for both individuals and societies is that it offers a threat to continuity in the lives of learners and the groups to which they belong. As we argued earlier, this threat can be diminished by the legitimizing capability of the formal system, which supports students and specifies, however loosely, their learning outcomes. Increased ease of access to the formal educational system at multiple points throughout life can help students maintain continuity in their lives.

A system of continuing education would provide instruction and support to all students, both part time and full time. In fact, the distinction between part-time and full-time students would cease to exist. There seems to be little academic basis for it, other than the full-time students' greater opportunity to enjoy the benefits of membership in the educational organization and culture. Recent studies (Long, 1986; Bettandorf, 1981) suggest that alterations in administrative practices could do much to improve the "membership" experience of students who study on something other than a formal, full-time basis.

A critical characteristic of a system of continuing education will be its ability to adjust continuously to what is taking place in the Learning Domain. In the past this adjustment has been slow, primarily because of the assumptions that learning was the exclusive prerogative of the educational system and that almost all learners were young and therefore were independent and incapable of autonomous choice. As we suggested earlier, the Educational Domain's adaptation to changes in the Learning Domain will be made quicker and easier if contact between them can be increased.

The "experiential learning" or "prior learning assessment" programs that we described in Chapter Six are an important exception to the lack of contact between the two domains. Such programs have been developing slowly but steadily in the United States, Britain, Canada, Sweden, and probably other advanced societies under different names. They assess learning accomplished outside of formal education as a basis for admission, placement, and certification within the formal system. They therefore represent an official recognition by the Educational Domain of learning accomplished in the Learning Domain.

PLA's potential for the reform of the formal educational system and for improvements in society's ability to manage learning is breathtaking. For one thing, it makes entrance to and exit from the formal educational system much easier and more flexible, thereby enhancing enormously education's genuinely "continuing" character. It also can help to ease the difficulties of "bridging the gap," that is, transferring young people from school to employment, or transferring adults temporarily from employment back to school for further education. Programs of "cooperative education" are already contributing to the solution of these problems, but prior learning assessment promises to provide a much more fundamental advance.

The conventional relationship of school and student has been that of a limited-term contract; that is, the student engaged with the agency for a specific time, after which each was through with the other. In the relationship implied by PLA and continuing education, however, a student would return regularly, over a period of many years, to an educational agency for new opportunities to learn about his or her profession or any other subject of interest. This new relationship would make the student less like the purchaser of a book and more like the subscriber to a magazine. PLA, cooperative education, and similar programs may restore the original meaning of stages, as distinct from completion, to academic terms such as *degree* and *graduation*.

The greatest importance of prior learning assessment, however, lies in its promise of allowing greater functional exchange between the Learning and Educational domains, which could lead to significant reform in the latter. Here also lies its greatest danger. Most advocates of prior learning assessment programs do not challenge the value of the certification controlled by the formal system. By implication, in fact, prior learning assessment enhances that value by extending certification even further across the Learning Domain. Instead of allowing the Learning Domain to penetrate, enliven, and reform the Educational Domain, therefore, prior learning assessment programs might simply help the Educational Domain "capture" the renewed vigor and scope of the Learning Domain by claiming that learning accomplished in the latter becomes valuable or significant only to the extent that it can be or has been assessed by the formal system. Such a destructive occurrence can be prevented only if the agencies of the Educational Domain respect the integrity of learners and the learning that they bring with them. Only if these agencies "listen" to the Learning Domain, constantly examining what they are teaching in the light of what is being learned elsewhere, will the gap be bridged effectively in both directions.

Another danger of these otherwise promising programs, as mentioned in Chapter Six, lies in possible deterioration of standards of assessment ("quality control"). Legitimate exchange of a complex learning experience, involving some form of "residence," for alternate symbols of learning accomplished, including learner-developed "portfolios" or other means of evaluation, is not impossible, but it does require skill and careful analysis. Evidence of that care has so far been encouraging, but maintaining it as the volume and scope of these programs increase will require great effort. Still, the objective of creating new relationships between the Learning and Educational domains is worth all the risks involved.

The modern world needs a newly conceived and defined system of education that can function effectively in societies based on the maximization of the human potential for learning. Most existing formal systems were designed for societies in which the demand for learning beyond childhood was confined to very small numbers of people. Those systems do not recognize that societal learning needs have changed and therefore do not understand why they have lost the public favor that they enjoyed so spectacularly only three decades ago. They also do not seem to recognize the need to redefine their purpose in order to meet these new needs.

Educational systems need to accept the fact that they are unlikely ever to recover their past domination of learning and control of learning resources. In contemporary and future societies, the Educational Domain inescapably will float in a sea of learning. Turbulence in that sea is unavoidable. The captains of the educational fleet will need new skills of navigation and, more important, the ability to identify new destinations for their vessels.

Creating a Learning Society

Throughout these arguments we have been hesitant to use the popular term "learning society." For one thing, as we have pointed out, only individuals learn. For another, although people can, do, and should learn throughout their lives, they do not learn constantly. We all have other things to do. Finally, learning is both exhilarating and frightening; it both requires and releases energy and courage. Learning means human beings facing themselves. Thus we can endure only so much learning at a time. For all these reasons, the notion that there could be a society in which every member is learning all the time is clearly an absurdity.

"Learning society" can have another meaning, however. It can mean a society that bases its very essence on the mobilization of the learning capacities of all of its citizens throughout all their lives. Obviously such a society remains a vision, something to be aspired to. Nowhere, to our knowledge, has anything like it been realized or even adequately conceived. It must be possible, however, for it is based on the most human of all human characteristics, the capacity to knowingly and willingly transform oneself. Along with loving, learning is our most promising endowment.

The foundations for a true learning society already exist. We know that the expression of the human urge to learn is influenced by, and in turn profoundly influences, social context. We have the capability to create collective environments that not only provide immeasurably more freedom for learning but depend for their survival on the full exercise of that new freedom. Creation of a learning society will not happen automatically, however, despite the powerful economic and technical forces that are pushing it toward birth. Opportunities for learning continue to be unevenly distributed among the world's population, and opposition to the freedom of learning remains strong in many quarters. We must strive for the full realization of every individual's learning potential, both because we know that we may destroy ourselves if we fail and because, if we succeed, the maximization of learning provides the most attractive and compelling vision of humankind. There can be no turning back.

References

Adams, R. J., Draper, P. M., and Ducharme, C. *Education and Working Canadians: Report of the Commission of Inquiry on Educational Leave and Productivity.* Ottawa: Labour Canada, 1979.

Ardrey, R. *The Territorial Imperative.* New York: Atheneum, 1966.

Ariyaratne, A. "Learning in Sarvodaya." In A. M. Thomas and E. Ploman (eds.), *Learning and Development: A Global Perspective.* Toronto: Ontario Institute for Studies in Education Press, 1986.

Baum, D. *The Final Plateau.* Toronto: Burns and MacEachern, 1974.

Beer, S. *Decision and Control.* London: Wiley, 1966.

Benderly, B. L. "The Great Ape Debate." *Science 80,* July-August 1980, pp. 61–65.

Berger, T. *Mackenzie Valley Pipeline Inquiry.* Ottawa: Ministry of Indian Affairs and Northern Development, Queen's Printer, 1976.

Bettandorf, R. "Adult Students Support Services." Unpublished doctoral dissertation, Department of Educational Administration, Counseling Psychology and Higher Education, University of Mississippi, 1981.

Blyth, J. A. *The Foundling at Varsity: Toronto School of Continuing Studies.* Toronto: University of Toronto, 1976.

Botkin, J., Elmandjra, M., and Maritza, M. *No Limits to Learning: Bridging the Human Gap.* Oxford, England: Pergamon Press, 1979.

185

Boulding, E. *The Place of the Family in Times of Social Transition: Imaging a Familial Future.* Vancouver: University of British Columbia, 1981.

Boulding, K. "Levels of Knowledge and Learning." In A. M. Thomas and E. Ploman (eds.), *Learning and Development: A Global Perspective.* Toronto: Ontario Institute for Studies in Education Press, 1986.

Boyer, E. *College: The Undergraduate Experience in America.* New York: Harper & Row, 1987.

Bridging the Gap. *Bridging the Gap Between Education and Employment,* 1988, *8* (1) (entire issue).

Brookfield, S. *Adult Learners, Adult Education and the Community.* New York: Teachers College Press, 1984.

Brown, G. E. *The Multi-problem Dilemma.* Metuchen, N.J.: Scarecrow Press, 1968.

Brundage, D., and MacKeracher, D. *Adult Learning Principles and Their Application to Program Planning.* Toronto: Ontario Institute for Studies in Education Press, 1980.

Bryson, L. "Notes on a Theory of Advice." In R. Merton (ed.), *A Reader in Bureaucracy.* New York: The Free Press of Glencoe, 1963.

Campbell, D. *The New Majority.* Edmonton: University of Alberta Press, 1984.

Canadian Association for Adult Education. *From the Adult's Point of View.* Toronto: Canadian Association for Adult Education, 1982.

Canada Department of Labour. *Apprenticeship in Canada.* Ottawa: Queen's Printer, 1953.

Carnevale, A. P., and Gainer, L. J. *The Learning Enterprise.* Washington, D.C.: The American Society for Training and Development/United States Department of Labor, Employment and Training Administration, 1989.

Carter, N. *Volunteers, The Untapped Potential.* Ottawa: Canadian Council for Social Development, 1975.

Clark, H. F., and Sloan, H. S. *Classrooms in the Factories.* Rutherford, N.J.: Institute of Research, Dickenson University, 1958.

Clark, H. F., and Sloan, H. S. *Classrooms in the Stores.* Sweet Springs, Mo.: Roxbury Press, 1962.

Clark, H. F., and Sloan, H. S. *Classrooms in the Military.* New York: Columbia University Press, 1964.

Clark, H. F., and Sloan, H. S. *Classrooms on Main Street.* New York: Teachers College Press, 1966.

Coady, M. M. *The Man from Margaree.* Toronto: McClelland & Stewart, 1971.

Counts, G. "Dare the Schools Build a New Social Order?" In R. Gross (ed.), *The Teacher and the Taught.* New York: Dell Publishers, 1963. (Originally published 1932.)

Cremin, L. *The American Common School.* New York: Teachers College Press, 1951.

Cremin, L. *The Transformation of the School.* New York: Knopf, 1961.

Curti, M. E. *The University of Wisconsin: A History 1848-1925.* Madison: University of Wisconsin Press, 1949.

Denys, L. "The Major Learning Efforts of Two Groups of Accra Adults." Unpublished doctoral dissertation, Division of Education, School of Graduate Studies, University of Toronto, 1973.

Department of University Extension and Continuing Studies. *A Piece of the Action.* St. John's, Newfoundland: Memorial University of Newfoundland, 1987.

Deutsch, K. *Nationalism and Social Communications.* Cambridge, Mass.: MIT Press, 1966.

Devereaux, M. S. *One in Every Five: A Survey of Adult Education in Canada.* Ottawa: Statistics Canada and the Education Support Sector, Secretary of State, 1985.

Dewey, J. *Democracy and Education.* New York: Macmillan, 1961.

Dore, R. *British Factory—Japanese Factory.* Berkeley, Calif.: University of California Press, 1973.

Dupre, J. *Federalism and Policy Development in Canada.* Toronto: University of Toronto Press, 1973.

Ellis, R. J. *Postsecondary Co-operative Education in Canada.* Ottawa: Science Council of Canada, 1987.

Ellul, J., *The Political Illusion.* New York: Knopf, 1967.

Eurich, N. P. *Corporate Classrooms: The Learning Business.* Lawrenceville, N.J.: The Carnegie Foundation for the Advancement of Teaching/Princeton University Press, 1985.

Fair, J. "Teachers as Learners." Unpublished doctoral dissertation, Division of Education, School of Graduate Studies, University of Toronto, 1973.

Faure, E. *Learning to Be: The World of Education, Today and Tomorrow.* Report to the International Commission on the Development of Education. Paris: UNESCO, 1973.

Federal Court of Appeal. *Renaissance International vs The Minister of National Revenue.* Ottawa: Federal Court of Appeal No. A–888–80, 1982.

Federal Court of Appeal. *Scarborough Community Legal Services vs Her Majesty the Queen.* Ottawa: Federal Court of Appeal Al–107–84, 1985.

Ferguson, M. *The Aquarian Conspiracy.* Los Angeles: Tarcher, 1980.

Fieldhouse, R. *The Workers' Educational Association: Aims and Achievements, 1903–1977.* Syracuse, N.Y.: Syracuse University, 1977.

Flesch, R. *Why Johnny Can't Read.* New York: Harper & Row, 1955.

Fournier, R. M. *Educational Brokering: The Women's Resource Centre Experience.* Vancouver: University of British Columbia, 1982.

Goodham-Smith, C. *The Great Hunger.* New York: Harper & Row, 1962.

Gordon, Com. W. L. *Report of the Royal Commission on Canada's Economic Prospects.* Ottawa: Queen's Printer, 1958.

Gould, S. *Diversity by Design.* San Francisco: Jossey-Bass, 1974.

Greater Toronto Southeast Asian Refugee Task Force. *Report of the Greater Toronto Southeast Asian Refugee Task Force.* Toronto: Social Planning Council of Metropolitan Toronto, 1981.

Hale, O. *The Captive Press in the Third Reich.* Princeton, N.J.: The Princeton University Press, 1964.

Hall, E. T. *Beyond Culture.* Garden City, N.Y.: Doubleday Anchor Press, 1976.

Herzberg, F. *Work and the Nature of Man.* Cleveland, Ohio: World, 1966.

Hewage, L. "Global Learning: East-West Perspectives with a Future Orientation." In A. M. Thomas and E. Ploman (eds.), *Learning and Development: A Global Perspective.* Toronto: Ontario Institute for Studies in Education Press, 1986.

Hiemstra, R. "Older Adult Learning: Instrumental and Expressive Categories." *Educational Gerontology,* 1979, *1* (3), 227–236.

olland, P. "Concept of Learning in the Study of Animal Behavior." In A. M. Thomas and E. Ploman (eds.), *Learning and Development: A Global Perspective.* Toronto: Ontario Institute for Studies in Education Press, 1986.

Homans, G. *The Human Group.* San Diego: Harcourt Brace Jovanovich, 1950.

Illich, I. *Deschooling Society.* London: Harper & Row, 1971.

"Industry Report: An Overview of Employee Training in America." *Training,* Oct. 1987, pp. 33–72.

Innis, H. A. *Empire and Communications.* Toronto: University of Toronto Press, 1972. (Originally published 1950.)

Jacobs, T., and Fuhrman, B. "The Concept of Learning Style." In J. W. Pfeiffer and L. D. Goodstein (eds.), *Developing Human Resources.* San Diego, Calif.: University Associates, 1984.

James, W. *The Varieties of Religious Experience.* New York: Collier, 1961.

Johnstone, J., and Rivera, R. *Volunteers for Learning.* Hawthorne, N.Y.: Aldine, 1965.

Joint Committee of University and Work. *Oxford and Working Class Education.* (2nd rev. ed.) Oxford: Clarendon Press, 1909.

Jutikkala, E. *A History of Finland.* London: Heinemann, 1979.

Kaplan, L. *Working with Multi-problem Families.* Toronto: Lexington Books, 1986.

Katz, E., and Lazarsfeld, P. F. *Personal Influence.* New York: Free Press, 1955.

Kegan, D. *The Foundations of Distance Education.* London: Croom Helm, 1986.

Kidd, J. R. *18 to 80.* Toronto: Board of Education for the City of Toronto, 1961.

Kidd, J. R. *How Adults Learn.* New York: Association Press, 1973.

Knowles, M. *The Adult Learner: A Neglected Species.* (3rd ed.) Houston: Gulf Publishing, 1984.

Kolb, D. *Experiential Learning.* Englewood Cliffs, N.J.: Prentice-Hall, 1984.

Kolm, R. *The Change of Cultural Identity.* New York: Arno Press, 1980.

Lasswell, H. D., Lerner, D., and Rothwell, C. E. *Comparative Study of Elites: An Introduction and Bibliography.* Stanford, Calif.: Stanford University Press, 1952.

Leary, T. *The Politics of Ecstasy.* New York: Putnam, 1968.

Levinson, D. *The Seasons of a Man's Life.* New York: Knopf, 1978.

Lewis, G. *Educating Rita.* Columbia Pictures, 1983.

Linden, B. *Apes, Men, and Language.* New York: Penguin Books, 1976.

Locke, J. *The Works of John Locke.* Aalen, Germany: Scientia Verlag, 1963. (Originally published 1823.)

Locke, J. *The Educational Writings of John Locke.* J. L. Axtell (ed.). London: Cambridge University Press, 1968.

Long, H. *Adult Learning: Research and Practice.* New York: Cambridge University Press, 1983.

Long, P. "Towards a Model of Institutional Supports for Part-Time Learning in Post-Secondary Education: Case Studies of Practice in Ontario, Canada, and Queensland, Australia." Unpublished doctoral dissertation, Department of Adult Education, Ontario Institute for Studies in Education, University of Toronto, 1986.

Lovell, R. B. *Adult Learning.* London: Croom Helm, 1980.

MacLeish, J. *The Ulyssean Adult: Creativity in the Middle and Later Years.* Toronto: McGraw-Hill/Ryerson, 1976.

McLuhan, M. *The Gutenberg Galaxy.* New York: New American Library, 1969.

Maslow, A. *Hierarchy, Motivation and Personality.* New York: Harper & Row, 1954.

Mead, M. *Coming of Age in Samoa.* New York: American Museum of Natural History, 1973.

Mezirow, J. "Perspective Transformation." *Adult Education,* 1978, 28 (2), 100–110.

Mezirow, J. "Perspective Transformation—Toward a Critical Theory of Adult Education." Lecture given at University of Illinois, Chicago, Sept. 1979.

Mugridge, I., and Kaufman, D. (eds.). *Distance Education in Canada.* London: Croom Helm, 1986.

National Advisory Committee on Voluntary Action. *People in*

Action: Report of the National Advisory Committee on Voluntary Action to the Government of Canada. Ottawa: Ministry of Supply and Services, 1978.

National Advisory Panel on Skill Development Leave. *Learning for Life: Overcoming the Separation of Work and Learning.* Ottawa: Ministry of Supply and Services, 1984.

Ohlinger, J. "Is Life Long Education a Guarantee of Permanent Inadequacy?" *Convergence,* 1974, *2,* 47–59.

Organization for Economic Cooperation and Development. *The Canadian Adult Training and Retraining Program.* Ottawa: Department of Manpower and Immigration, Planning and Evaluation Branch, 1968.

Ouchi, W., and Jaeger, A. "Type Z Corporation: Stability in the Midst of Mobility." Academy of Management Review, 1978, *3* (2), 305–314.

Oxford Illustrated Dictionary. London: Oxford University Press, 1975.

Pavlov, I. P. *Conditioned Reflexes.* (G. V. Anrep, trans. and ed.) New York: Dover Publications, 1960. (Originally published 1927.)

Penfield, W. *Speech and Brain Mechanisms.* Princeton, N.J.: Princeton University Press, 1959.

Perry, W. *The Open University.* San Francisco: Jossey-Bass, 1977.

Peters, T., and Waterman, R. H. *In Search of Excellence: The Culture of Organizations.* New York: Harper & Row, 1982.

Pietsch, P. "The Mind of a Microbe." *Science Digest,* October 1983, pp. 70–71, 103.

Podoluk, J. R. *Incomes of Canadians.* Ottawa: Dominion Bureau of Statistics, 1968.

Rakoff, V. "The Inescapable Family." Paper presented at 20th anniversary conference of the Zanier Institute for the Family, Ottawa, Oct. 1985.

Rashdall, H. *The Universities of Europe in the Middle Ages.* Oxford: Clarendon Press, 1936.

"Read It and Weep: Questions and Results of a Science Quiz to Test Science Literacy." *Globe and Mail,* Mar. 1, 1990, p. 7.

Richmond, H. *Statesmen and Sea Power.* Oxford: Clarendon Press, 1946.

Saint, A. *Learning at Work: Human Resources and Organizational Development.* Chicago: Nelson-Hall, 1974.

Schon, D. *Beyond the Stable State.* London: Maurice Temple Smith, 1971.

Scribner, S., and Cole, M. *The Psychology of Literacy.* Cambridge, Mass.: Harvard University Press, 1981.

Sheehy, G. *Passages: Predictable Crises of Adult Life.* New York: Dutton, 1976.

Skill Development Leave Task Force. *Learning a Living in Canada.* Ottawa: Minister of Supply and Services, 1983.

Skinner, B. F. *Science and Human Behavior.* New York: Macmillan, 1953.

Smullen, I. "The Chimp that Went Fishing." *International Wildlife,* May-June 1978, pp. 17–18.

Steinberg, S. *Five Hundred Years of Printing.* London: Penguin, 1974.

Stock, A., Duke, C., Gundara, A., and Thomas, A. M. "Three Commonwealth Country Studies of the Educational Provisions for New Entrants." Unpublished manuscript, Commonwealth Foundation, London, 1986.

Sutherland, H. "The In-Service Education of Managers in Selected Japanese and Canadian Organizations." Unpublished doctoral dissertation, Department of Adult Education, Ontario Institute for Studies in Education, University of Toronto, 1986.

Thomas, A. M., Abbey, D. S., and MacKeracher, D. *Labour Canada's Labour Education Program: The First Four Years.* Ottawa: Labour Canada, 1982.

Thomas, A. M., Abbey, D. S., and MacKeracher, D. *Evaluation of the Federal Government's Labour Education Program.* Ottawa: Labour Canada, 1983.

Thomas, A. M., Beatty, D., Ironside, D. J., and Herman, R. *Learning in Organizations: Four Case Studies of Education in Industry.* Toronto: Department of Adult Education, Ontario Institute for Studies in Education, University of Toronto, 1980.

Thomas, A. M., and Klaiman, R. *The Mature Student in the Secondary School in Ontario.* Toronto: Secondary School Teachers Federation, 1988.

Thomas, A. M., MacKeracher, D., MacNeil, T., and Selman,

G. *Adult Learning About Canada.* Ottawa: Department of the Secretary of State, 1982.

Thomas, A. M., and others. *New Reflections on the Learning Society.* Toronto: Department of Adult Education, Ontario Institute for Studies in Education, University of Toronto, 1981.

Thomas, W. I., and Znaniecki, F. *The Polish Peasant in Europe and America.* New York: Octagon Books, 1974.

Thorndike, E. *Adult Learning.* New York: Macmillan, 1935.

Tough, A. "Major Learning Efforts: Recent Research and Future Directions." *Adult Education,* 1978, *18* (4), 250–263.

Tough, A. M. *The Adult's Learning Experience.* (2nd ed.) Toronto: Ontario Institute for Studies in Education Press, 1979.

Trevelyan, G. M. *History of England.* London: Longmans, 1945.

United Nations Educational, Scientific, and Cultural Organization (UNESCO). *Declaration of Fourth International Conference on Adult Education.* Paris: UNESCO, 1985.

United States Training Census and Trends Report. New York: Geller Publishing, 1982.

United States Training Census and Trends Report. New York: Geller Publishing, 1983.

United States Training Census and Trends Report. New York: Geller Publishing, 1984.

Vanier, J. *Community and Growth, Our Pilgrimage Together.* Toronto: Griffin House, 1979.

Waddell, H. J. *The Wandering Scholars.* New York: Holt, Rinehart & Winston, 1927.

Waddell, H. J. *Peter Abelard.* London: Constable, 1933.

Waniewicz, I. *The Demand for Part-time Learning in Ontario.* Toronto: Ontario Educational Communications Authority and Ontario Institute for Studies in Education Press, 1976.

Waples, D., Berelson, B., and Bradshaw, F. *What Reading Does to People.* Chicago: The University of Chicago Press, 1940.

Wells, H. G., *The Outline of History.* London: Cassell, 1920.

Williams, J. *Byng of Vimy.* London: Secker and Warburg, 1983.

Wolfe, T. *You Can't Go Home Again.* New York: Harper & Row, 1940.

Young, W. R. "Making the Truth Graphic: The Canadian Government's Home Front Information Structure and Program During World War II." Unpublished doctoral dissertation, Department of Adult Education, University of British Columbia, 1978.

Index

195